Ports of Call

Ports of Call

♦

Journeys in Ministry

Richard D. Leonard
Minister Emeritus
Unitarian Church of All Souls
New York City

10/10/04

*To Ruth —
With warmest regards
and thanks for your interest
in our liberal heritage.*

Dick Leonard

iUniverse, Inc.
New York   Lincoln   Shanghai

Ports of Call
Journeys in Ministry

All Rights Reserved © 2004 by Richard Leonard

No part of this book may be reproduced or transmitted in any form or by any means, graphic, electronic, or mechanical, including photocopying, recording, taping, or by any information storage retrieval system, without the written permission of the publisher.

iUniverse, Inc.

For information address:
iUniverse, Inc.
2021 Pine Lake Road, Suite 100
Lincoln, NE 68512
www.iuniverse.com

Cover design by Mike Quon, Quon Design, 543 River Road, Fair Haven, N.J. 07744

ISBN: 0-595-30619-5

Printed in the United States of America

Contents

Foreword	vii
Sermons	
One Degree of Separation——2000	1
I'll Be Damned——1999	12
Insider-Outsider——1998	19
One Life——1996	29
A View From the Bottom——1994	36
One Leg at a Time——1992	43
In the Name of Allah——1991	52
When Death Comes Home——1990	60
What Dizzy Dean Taught Me——1989	68
The Great Strainer of Naturalness——1987	77
Frozen Bow Ties——1981	87
From the Quarterly	
Rest in Peace——1989	96
Birthday Party for a Hundred-Year-Old——1989	99
A Weekend in My Life——1987	101
Poems	
The Sunday Before Christmas——1993	104
The Modern Unitarian——1993	106

Annual Report
    To the Congregation——1998   108

And
    The Day the Russians Came——1990   110
        by Dick Leonard
    The Day the Russians Went Home——1990   118
        by Bruce Clear

Epilogue——2004   127

Acknowledgements   *131*

About the Author   *133*

Foreword

In the forty-eighth year of my ministry, it was suggested by Forrest Church that I put together some of my favorite sermons for publication under one cover.

Thinking first of our five children, seven grandchildren, and four great-grandchildren—all of whom in future decades might like to have such a piece to refer to—but thinking also of the congregation of All Souls in New York, our wonderfully accepting church home for the past twenty-four years, which has urged me to preach more often than I have been inclined to do, I decided to assemble a group of sermons and other writings representing my time at All Souls, and this book is the result.

If one theme runs through these writings, it is that this world is a vaster place than any of us can imagine, with tremendous variations of culture and human experience. Yet the human community is essentially one, physically, and tied into the interdependent but fragile web that sustains all life.

As I read these materials I am also struck by how much humor crept into my writings, which I hope the reader will stumble on again and again. It comes not from a belief that life is uniformly funny. Indeed, many experiences in life are so painful one wants instinctively to bury them and never revisit them.

But I've also learned how often the very painful experience comes back to us, in time, as almost pure comedy. For proof, perhaps the reader should start at page 110, "The Day the Russians Came."

I want to thank Polly, who has put up with a somewhat "antic" but loving husband for thirty-three years, and my colleagues, Forrest

Church, Galen Guengerich, and Jan Carlsson-Bull, who continually furnish support.

Special mention should be made of Scott Will, Alison Collins and Megan Martin for their work on this manuscript.

I must also express my deepest appreciation to the Rev. Bruce Clear, now of the All Souls Unitarian Church of Indianapolis, for giving permission to include in this book his delightful account of The Day the Russians Went Home. It completes the epic adventure of fourteen young Russians who went almost around the world twice in two weeks to be with new friends in the United States. The first leg of their journey led to my writing The Day the Russians Came.

And, finally I thank our five beautiful, accomplished and inspiring children: Suzy, Elizabeth, Helen Louise, Ken and Martha. This book is for you.

D.

Sermons

ONE DEGREE OF SEPARATION

READING

"A Prayer for Older People"
Anonymous; contributed by Christine Mayer

Lord, thou knowest that I am growing older.
Keep me from becoming talkative and possessed with the
   idea that I must express myself on every subject.
Release me from the craving to straighten out everybody's
   life.
Keep my mind free from the recital of endless detail.
Give me wings to get to the point and then be quiet.
Seal my lips when I am inclined to tell my aches and pains.
They are increasing with the years, and my love to speak of
   them grows sweeter as time goes by.
Make me thoughtful but not nosy—helpful but not bossy.
With my vast store of wisdom and experience, it does seem
   a pity not to use it all, but thou knowest, Lord, that I
   want a few friends at the end.

SERMON
June 11, 2000

The year was 1988.

Polly and I had already been at All Souls for about ten years. She was working at Citibank. We had developed the custom by then of taking whatever vacation time we could put together for a whole year, and using it to go as far from New York City as funds and time would permit. In fact, we sacrificed many amenities all year long so that we could travel. In eighteen years we had already been as far away as China, India and Egypt.

But in 1988 we had the wild idea of going all though the vastness of Russia, out to Siberia, and down into Mongolia. Gorbychev had taken the reins of his government, and the key words were *glasnost* and *peristroika*. It seemed like a good time to see that part of the world.

Polly and I are often asked the question, "Of all the places you have seen, what is your favorite place in the world?" That's an impossible question for us to answer. But if the question is put differently, "What single event in your travels stands out as the most unusual or rewarding?" we would probably agree that it was the night of May 25, 1988, at a yurt camp on the Gobi Desert in Mongolia. The events that evening give rise to the title of this sermon, "One Degree of Separation."

We had flown from Moscow to Novosibirsk, deep in the Ural Mountains, then to Irkutsk in Eastern Siberia. We had seen the world's biggest dam at Bratsk and boarded the Trans-Siberian Railway for the journey to Ulan Bator, the capital of Outer Mongolia.

We had spent two nights in a yurt camp in the Gobi Desert. (Yurts, incidentally, are those uniquely Mongolian round tents made of wood strips and animal hides, with a stove in the middle and a pipe leading up through a flap in the top of the tent. The yurt can be moved easily by camels around the countryside. It takes about six hours to put up a yurt, with its wooden floor and furniture, and about two hours to take it down and load it on the backs of four camels. Today, heavy factory-made plastic is used in place of animal hides. Otherwise, it is a way of life that has not changed in thousands of years.)

Mongolia considers itself a Communist country, with all the land belonging to all the people. Consequently, yurts are put up anywhere they are desired, including the middle of Ulan Bator, even in its central square. We were continually finding yurts in improbable places.

We had spent two nights in the desert and flown back to Ulan Bator for a tour of that interesting place, with its modern theater and hotel and ancient Buddhist shrines and monasteries. I had managed to dislocate a shoulder, and had also begun to develop a hernia. The two things in a strange way offset each other.

Then we flew off to a second camp in the desert, at a place called Khujirt, for a one-night stay on the 24th. We were to fly back on the 25th.

Keep in mind, when I talk about flying, these were not large planes. They were propeller-driven and could just hold our party of fourteen Americans and a few traveling Mongolians and people of other countries. The runways in the desert were unpaved, semi-hard strips of sand, with a certain amount of up-and-down roll to them. It was unnerving to watch a plane coming toward the landing strip, see its wheels touch down, and then see it disappear altogether in a trough, only to rise up again and stop in front of you.

On the night of the 24th, we had dinner in a very large yurt, along with other groups of tourists. There might well have been a hundred people eating together, but we were very much in our separate groups. The menu, very sparse to begin with in Mongolia, included a stew of yak meat and beans or potatoes.

Polly and I went to bed that night in our individual family yurt, which was actually capable of handling four couples. But since this was not the heaviest season for tourists, we had the yurt to ourselves and we were very comfortable.

At three o'clock in the morning, nature called us both at about the same time, and we set out on foot for the combination washhouse and latrine, which was not exactly close-by, perhaps at a distance of a city block.

The moment we emerged from our tent, we were struck by the intense beauty of the sky overhead with its zillions of stars that one could never see except where there is no competing light. In this case, a single light bulb in the distance pointed us toward the washhouse. I wished that even it could be turned off briefly so that we could feel more a part of the sky than a part of the world. The vision of the sky at 3 a.m., on that warm evening in the desert, will remain with us forever.

But that is not the story.

Four hours later we got up again, opened the door of our yurt, and were absolutely stunned to see that it was snowing, where a few hours before we had looked up at the clear starry night. Such are the changes of weather in the desert. It continued to snow, and the snow stuck to the desert sand. Jokes were told at breakfast about Santa coming down our stovepipes.

The plane that was to take us back to Ulan Bator could not land in that weather, so most of the day was spent guessing whether or when we would leave. Meanwhile, we did little walking tours of the town. I remember at one point entertaining twenty or thirty children with my Rubik's Cube, a big curiosity in those days.

The snow turned to rain, and because of the bad weather the airplane never came. We were faced with an unexpected second night in the camp. Dinner was eaten rather quietly by the various groups in our big dining yurt.

Meanwhile, an idea was percolating in Polly's head, to which, when she put it to me, my reaction was, "Preposterous!" The gist of her idea was this: "Here we have these various groups in camp at the same time, and no one is speaking to anyone outside of their own group. We eat in the same room, we watch the German women splash ice cold water on themselves in the johns, we sometimes smile at each other, but nobody is able to really communicate outside his or her group. Now we are faced with an evening with no planned program. There must be some way we can break the ice, literally, and interact with each other!"

I said, "Preposterous," because the language hurdle just seemed too immense. Polly persisted and began talking with our guide, Mara Koltanov, whose initial reaction wasn't far from mine.

But Mara was a delightful young woman who fortunately spoke Russian, Mongolian, English and German.

Mara rounded up the four of five other guides, who spoke a variety of languages, and convinced them that Polly's idea was at least worth a try. They still had to convince their own constituencies that they should leave their warm yurts and return to the dining-hall yurt, for what could be a complete catastrophe in international relations.

But return we did. For one thing, there wasn't much else to do—even the stars were hidden by the heavy clouds. The groups trooped back into the big yurt. Their faces betrayed that they shared my dire foreboding.

With the guides acting as a team at the front of the yurt, we Americans found ourselves asking ourselves painful questions, like "What can we ask another group that won't offend them? If people sing, what song do we Americans have in common that we could possibly sing, given the diversity in *our* group?"

We learned that we were five groups of people in camp. Three were Russian, one was German, and the fourteen of us were from the United States. The three Russian groups were as diverse as the rest of us. One group was from Khabarovsk, near Vladivostok on the far eastern end of Siberia; one was from Saratov on the Volga River in Western Europe; and the third was a group of performers from Alma Ata, deep in the southern part of Kazakhstan. The Germans were East German, from a place fittingly called Karlmarxstadt.

The Americans managed to convey to the Alma Atans that we had been scheduled to see Alma Ata, but that the itinerary had been changed at the last minute and we were only able to see their city from a distance.

The Alma Atans agreed to start things off. Three of them welcomed the rest of us rather formally, in Russian of course, with our several guides translating. So far, so good!

A young Alma Atan girl then sang a song, with the rest of their group responding in song. Then they presented a duet. They continued to sing and did a folk dance.

Meanwhile, panic had gripped the Americans. What would we do? We couldn't even agree on a simple song to sing.

An effort was made at questions and answers around the room. All laughed when someone asked why we Americans seemed so much older than everyone in the room. We came up with two answers: (a) we had to work a long time to afford a trip like this, and (b) we had to travel so far, we aged some just in getting there.

We asked questions about why the Eastern Siberians were visiting Mongolia. It turned out that four of them paid their own way, but the others were being honored because they were the best workers in their plant.

The Americans caucused and decided that I should take the bull by the horns—I would represent them and sing my comic song "Foolish Questions." The song is supposed to pull the audience into responding to each foolish question with a perfectly obvious answer. But how would it work in a multi-language situation?

I told everybody that the Americans didn't know the song, but would respond to my questions. Off I went, without benefit of the customary guitar or ukulele. Polly tried to lead the Americans in vigorous responses, but the responses were pretty weak.

At the end, I realized that the song had been a great hit with everybody, while only a few people grasped the words. Fortunately, I had a new idea—I would recite the song without music very slowly as if it were a poem, while Mara translated into Russian. The East German guide could get the drift, then whisper it to her people.

So I recited the song, very slowly. Now the Russians were howling with laughter. Unfortunately, the East German guide was overwhelmed, and the East German group sat glumly watching the rest of us laugh.

At least the Americans had come through with something. Abe, in our group, tried to follow up, telling a bad joke about an army general and a lack of water. When water is at last found in the story, the general announces, "The good news is: you can now change your underwear—the bad news is: only with each other."

That brought more discussion than laughter, in four languages, as people tried to figure out the import of the joke. Polly yelled to Abe, over the hubbub, "I don't even get it myself!"

The Russians from Saratov, on the Volga, took their turn. The city is across the river from the city of Engles. Yuri Gagarin completed his first-man-in-space flight right there at Saratov. They proudly handed around postcards with scenes from Saratov, and pictures of Gagarin, who apparently put their town on the map.

The East Germans took their turn, but "copped out" by having their bus driver, a Mongolian, sing. He had an operatic voice and had probably been serenading them on the bus all the way from the Russian boarder.

The performers from Alma Ata gave gifts to the Mongolian camp director, including a set of postcards and a lovely dish.

The camp director then asked whether we preferred Mongolian or western food. The Americans answered in one voice, "Mongolian!" Of course, he was asking about which we preferred in his camp. But I heard the question differently, as in "If you had to spend the rest of your life eating yak meat in its various forms, or western food with its infinite cuisines, which would you prefer?" Of course, I opened my mouth to say, "Western!" but nothing came out. I couldn't believe I heard the Americans shout "Mongolian!"

Our group asked the Russians from Saratov to sing "The Volga Boatman," and they politely refused. We thought we had offended them. Did they regard the song as a stereotype and want to distance themselves from it? Not at all, it turned out. It was simply that they were mostly women (we hadn't noticed), and they felt they couldn't do the song justice without some heavy male voices.

The question was put, "Would you like to visit the United States some day?" From all corners of the tent came a resounding "Yes!"

Suddenly we heard three young women's voices singing together. We didn't know who was singing. Then we saw. In a booth were three young Mongolian women, singing for us in their language. We hadn't known they were there. We were six groups, not five! After hearty applause for them, we all found ourselves singing "Ah, Chachonia," if not raising the roof, at least raising the stovepipe flap.

The Americans had one more ace up their sleeve. We had found a song we all knew. Full-throated, and with no reservation whatever, we belted out in four-part harmony, no less, "Let Me Call You Sweetheart." We may not have reached the level of the Sundowners Barbershop Quartet in our rendition, but we reached a level that has not been heard before or since in Outer Mongolia.

As the evening was drawing to a close, the camp director took a turn at the microphone again. Speaking in Mongolian, his only language, and rapidly translated into German, Russian and English, he told us that this evening fulfilled a dream of his. For sixteen years he had watched groups from many countries come and go from his camp, and that never had he seen an evening like this, with so much good will between people of different backgrounds. And he profoundly thanked us.

And today I profoundly thank my wife for not knowing the meaning of the word *preposterous* when it came to reaching out to other people.

By the way, the evening ended with dancing in the main yurt, a great deal of hand-shaking, and words uttered without thought as to whether they were understood. I made sure the Russians knew that chess was my game as well as theirs.

Later, in our yurt, with the door open to let in the cool night air, an East German woman came by and left us a colored booklet of her city, Karlmarxstadt, of which she was obviously very proud. We gave her all that we could think of in the way of a meaningful present—a handful of Citibank ballpoint pens, and she treated them as though they were the perfect gift.

As I said in the beginning of my sermon, many interesting things have happened to Polly and me in thirty years of traveling.

We have felt very close to nature at times, with the animals of Africa, the heat of the Valley of Kings, the cold winds of Norway's Cape. We have even come close to being killed on a few occasions. Our plane was once hit by lightning; another time we had to climb out of a Land Rover in full view of three lions 800 feet away.

But in spite of all the vagaries of travel, like getting food poisoning, or even having a hernia and a shoulder separation on the same trip, the events that really stand out in our minds are the encounters with people; both the people we have traveled with and the people whose countries we have visited. Again and again we are struck with the overwhelming friendliness of people when they are not caught up in ideological conflict.

Twenty-eight years ago a man in Frankfurt, Germany, saw us on a main street exhausted and unable to get a cab to our hotel. He picked up our bags, one under each arm, and ran with them a half-mile to the hotel, deposited them at the doorway, and ran off before we could even thank him.

More recently a good Samaritan in Warsaw discovered our passports in a trash can and returned them to our hotel without leaving his or her name, even though the passports were worth $10,000 each on the black market.

We remember the family in Budapest that waited for us for six hours in the railroad station, even though we were that late, to take us to their house and share a meal with us.

And so it goes, on and on, people encounters, from which we learned that we are not separated from each other by six degrees, as the story and play suggest, but by the single degree of being individual human beings.

In college, my greatest interest was certainly in the humanities, particularly sociology and anthropology: how people lived together in different societies, why they went to war, how they kept the peace, how institutions evolved over tens of thousands of years, differently in different places.

But I also had to take some physical science courses, such as physics and zoology, just to complete the requirements for a degree, and I found those courses somewhat harder.

One thing I took away from my zoology course, where we studied in great detail how human organs function in relation to the total body, was summed up by the professor when he said, "If you go just below the very surface of every human being, that is, the very thinnest layer of pigment that gives us our skin color, for every way that humans are different from one another, they are like each other in a thousand ways."

That means that if I go to Asia or Africa or Australia and shake hands with the first stranger I meet, be he or she of royal lineage or of untouchable caste, rich or poor, meticulously clean or indescribably dirty, that person is, from a biological point of view, a mirror of myself by a factor of a thousand to one. Unfortunately, our eyes pick up the differences that are only on the surface.

I guess the other thing I permanently learned in zoology was that each human body is a complete miracle of composition and function, so detailed as to make the most finely crafted mechanical construction, the Hubbell Telescope for example, look like a piece of junk by comparison.

I pick up a newspaper and read that some elderly woman has been stabbed to death in her apartment by an unknown assailant. The temptation may be to say, "Well, she was elderly, she pretty much had lived her life, she should have been more careful," and so forth.

But immediately my mind goes back to Zoology 101. Here was a functioning miracle of creation! A being as complicated as I am in every way, who felt each stab just as I would feel it if I were this victim, and who watched her life, her only life, slipping away, slipping away.

I believe that we do not think enough about that single degree of separation that differentiates us from all other humans and the fact that it is only one degree, biologically and sociologically, that puts us all in the same lifeboat.

The Mongolian bus driver who sang like Pavarotti that night, no matter how good his voice actually was, *was* Pavarotti, by a factor of a thousand to one.

The three little girls who finally got up the courage to sing, when nobody noticed them, could have been right out of our church school.

The stranger at coffee hour downstairs could be you or me at our first coffee hour.

As Maya Angelou says in her poem "Human Family":

I've sailed upon the Seven Seas
And stopped in every land;
I've seen the wonders of the world,
Not yet one 'common' man....

We seek success in Finland,
Are born and die in Maine.
In minor ways we differ,
In major, we're the same.

I note the obvious differences
Between each sort and type.
But we are more alike, my friends,
Than we are unalike.

I'll Be Damned

READING

If, recognizing the interdependence of all life, we strive to build community, the strength we gather will be our salvation. If you are black and I am white, it will not matter.

If you are female and I am male, it will not matter. If you are older and I am younger, it will not matter. If you are progressive and I am conservative, it will not matter. If you are straight and I am gay, it will not matter.

If you are Christian and I am Jewish, it will not matter. If we join spirits as brothers and sisters, the pain of aloneness will be lessened, and that does matter. In this spirit we build community and move toward restoration.

—The Rev. Marjorie Bowens-Wheatley

SERMON
June 13, 1999

Some of the best stories I've heard over the years come from my rabbi friends.

One rabbi, whom I'll call Harold, told me about once having been part of a large religious council composed of ministers, rabbis and priests. It was recognized as a very effective council. Its members got along well together as they worked on important community projects.

But there was a kind of unwritten premise in the organization that theology would not be discussed. So they didn't. And it worked.

Then one day they began to look at that underlying premise critically. And basically they said, "After all, we are theologians, to one degree or another. Theology is presumably our most important concern. Why shouldn't we be able to, and want to, discuss among ourselves the matters that are closest to our hearts?"

So they set a date when they would come together only to discuss theology, in a reasonable format.

That day came, the discussion took place and it began to get fairly heated. At one point Harold and a minister friend found themselves each standing, addressing the other. Harold said, "Now John, let me get this straight. Here we've been friends all these years, we've worked on the same projects, and you are saying to me that unless I accept exactly your interpretation of Jesus as my personal savior, I am damned to hell through all eternity when I die?"

And his minister friend said, "Harold, with all due respect to you, and you're a marvelous man and we've fought for the same causes and I have nothing but the highest regard for you, yes, that is exactly what I believe."

And Harold said he was surprised to hear himself say, as he sat down, "Well, I'll be damned."

Whenever I've told that story I've gotten an explosive reaction. It proves to me that theology is a very live issue for all of us. Under the surface of daily activity there is a very deep concern for such things as the nature of God, for who gets damned and who doesn't get damned, where exactly Jesus fits into the scheme of the universe, and how we conduct ourselves in the face of those with very different opinions.

In fact, when you think about it, 'damnation' really isn't a funny subject at all. A child born in the Sudan today, and in many places of the world, has a life expectancy of a few months to maybe several years. Any of us could have been born just as easily into that situation. Can we, for more than a few seconds, contemplate the life of a six-year-old dying of starvation as if it were our own life? If we want to use the word *damnation*, it seems to me to best befit the lives of children who have no hope.

The word applies suitably to other situations, such as the family forced from their home and all their possessions and made to march endless miles, perhaps separated forever from loved ones. Or the person in such physical pain that he or she can only wish the next moment were the last. Or the person whose mind and emotions are so scrambled that nothing can make sense any more.

'Damnation' is not pretty, and we can find it all around us and even catch glimpses in ourselves of what a living hell might be for us.

This in a world that for most of us, most of the time I'm convinced, runs from benign to wonderful. Just being able to look at a tree in bloom, or at someone returning a smile, or in eating a super-rich dessert (or just thinking about eating a super-rich dessert), life is full of one happy surprise after another for most people, punctuated by the occasional downer that we learn to cope with.

The reason the story of the rabbi and his minister friend is so funny is that it says that the ideas of heaven and hell can become so abstract, even for clergy, that they have no connection to everyday life.

That's the irony of most religion, it seems to me. Religion, which should be the great unifier of people, which in every case attempts to set out the highest aspirations of a people, be they Muslims, Christians, Jews or whatever, in its institutional form tends to divide people, not only Christians against Jews or Muslims, but Christians against Christians, and Jews against Jews, and Muslims against Muslims.

I'm convinced that the reason most people don't join religious institutions is that they see this aspect of institutionalized religion all too clearly, and they want no part of it. It takes a particular kind of vision, and I think a lot of Unitarian Universalists have caught it, that says that how we act toward one another is the measure of our religion, not what we say in our loftiest or most opinionated statements.

Joan Campbell, director of the National Council of Churches, reports that at a recent conference on abortion involving leading spokespersons from various faiths, a Roman Catholic cleric explained at the end why he personally opposed abortion. But then he had the grace to say, "I offer this statement as the deeply-held belief of my church. But I also offer this statement with the deep conviction that I might be wrong."

What a remarkable thing for him to say! For anyone to say! "These are my strong beliefs. But I just might be wrong."

Such a person is really willing to listen to a different point of view, engage in civil discourse, and be changed if logic dictates.

More often we are changed not by logic but by simply experiencing the other person or culture. We are thrown into a situation where we are no longer in control. We sit in a classroom where the children take charge. Or in a catastrophe we find ourselves working shoulder to shoulder with someone whose path we normally would never have crossed. At a dinner party we find ourselves suddenly outnumbered by people with radically different values and life styles. It's happened to all of us.

Many of you may have caught the May 23, 1999, *New York Times* Week in Review Section, with its page of excerpts written by students of Columbine High School in Littleton, Colorado, who had survived the massacre that spring. I found all of the excerpts illuminating and to the point of who we are and what we should be doing.

Janelle Behan, one of the students, wrote, "At first when this happened, people kept telling me that 'everything happens for a reason.' That made me so angry! How could there ever be a reason for something like this to happen, and what good could ever come of it? Well, as each day goes by now, I am seeing more and more good that is coming from it....

"Some of the good began even before everything was over, while I was still in the choir office with sixty other students. There were people I hardly knew who were comforting me, hugging me, and telling me that everything was going to be OK. There was a group of about six boys who literally saved all our lives. If it hadn't been for all of them, none of us would have known what to do. It was kind of funny, because many of these boys are thought of as goofy kids in everyday life. But they had taken the panels out of the ceiling to lift girls through who couldn't breathe, and they kept all of us quiet so that we couldn't be heard outside. I learned that many of the people at the school whom I thought I really didn't like, I love them all!"

Patricia Doyle wrote, "I do not believe I will ever understand what those horrible boys were thinking. That is what bugs me most, what were they thinking! This tragedy, though, has taught me many things.

"The way I live my life has come into my head many times. Am I doing the right thing always? Am I making people feel bad by the way I am treating them? I know joking is part of life, but I will never make fun of someone jokingly again. I hope many kids see, instead of just hearing about it, how much teasing can hurt a person."

As a clergy person, I'm glad that many of the young people, in Littleton and elsewhere, are waking up to the fact that what we say to other people, and words that imply rejection, can come back to haunt us, and even exact a price.

I hope they realize, too, that even more important than words, spoken in jest or otherwise, are the underlying attitudes we have about people, which are transmitted like poison darts, or like rays of sunshine, without our hardly being aware of what they say.

This past March Polly and I had the opportunity of spending three weeks on the west coast of Africa, sailing from Cape Town up past Gibraltar to Italy, and stopping in countries whose names we knew, like Namibia, Benin, Togo, Ghana, Ivory Coast, and Senegal, before visiting more familiar places like the Canary Islands and Morocco.

It was a remarkable vacation, and we learned a lot. Now we can at least picture each of those countries as an entity, some French-speaking in addition to their native tongues, some English-speaking like Ghana and more oriented toward England and the United States, some heavily Muslim in their culture and religion, others like Togo and Benin, most influenced by voodooism.

Indeed, Benin is considered the birthplace and the seat of voodooism. From Benin it spread to other African countries, but particularly to the Caribbean though the slave trade. It is a religion that is every bit as serious to its practitioners as is Christianity to Christians or Islam to Muslims.

Moreover, while I have not come to terms with the level of scientific understanding of the voodoo priest, who uses the skulls of animals, the skins of monkeys, or other animal viscera to effect his cures, a part of me warmly resonates to the idea that there is a 'spirit' in every living thing, from the giant oak to the ant that crawls on it, and in all inanimate objects as well. In voodooism, this church building has a spirit, and it is up to us to keep it a 'well' spirit, or help heal it if it becomes sick.

But there is one aspect of our trip to West Africa that troubled me then and continues to trouble me today.

Polly and I, and I dare say just about everyone on the Pacific Princess, felt we were on a goodwill mission, as well as a great vacation, hoping to gain understanding of a part of the world that doesn't have a lot of visitors from North America. Cotonou, Benin, located almost on the Equator, doesn't see many passenger ships during a year, as compared to South and East Africa, with their popular animal photo safaris.

Our ship was modest, especially compared to the megaships that are being built today to accommodate the upsurge in world sea travel. But I have to tell you that our medium-size Pacific Princess must have been easily the biggest floating object a lot of people in West Africa had ever seen.

So the piers were decked out waiting for us, with some of the finest art objects the continent could sell to tourists. The dancers danced on the pier, the drums beat until they rang in our heads, and native costumes outdid one another.

I'm sure we created an image of a boatload of helplessly wealthy North Americans on a sight-seeing trip of a very poor continent indeed.

Forget that Abidjan on the Ivory Coast is a metropolis in surprising ways, with more than a million people, skyscrapers, and lovely hotels and parkways. In the shadow of one hotel hundreds of men who could not get jobs in their home country of Mali and had migrated to the Ivory Coast, did the laundry of the better-off in the river, and laid out thousands of garments on the hillside to dry, without any apparent problem of laundry getting mixed up or lost.

Forget that we had come to West Africa with a thirst to know more about the slave trade, and that we visited the dungeons where for almost 300 years slaves were held, separated from their families, awaiting shipment overseas under the most cruel conditions, which guaranteed that a large percentage of them would die on the trip.

Forget that we did spend some money, but for trinkets, because we don't have room for anything more in our New York City apartment.

Forget these things, because the contrast was too great.

As out ship inched away from the pier in Dakar, where we had visited the Ile de Goree, the most notorious of all slavery centers, the merchants on the pier were putting their wares into their vehicles. The drums and the dancing stopped. One merchant made a gesture of "Good riddance!" I don't know how much he had expected to sell to all those rich Westerners that day, but he obviously had fallen short of his expectations.

I wondered then, as I wonder now, what it will take to save a dying continent where AIDS runs rampant, and the list of diseases alone is frightening. We know we can no more cut Africa off our conscience than our own country can cut off New York or California.

We are all in the same leaky boat, folks!

I started out with a light-hearted story of a rabbi hearing himself say, "Well, I'll be damned."

I end with the thought that in the long run, we may all be damned if we don't do everything we can to make bridges between cultures and religions and economic groups.

There are people of goodwill in all countries, by the millions, even by the billions. If we are to avoid the harsh judgment of history, and great suffering for ourselves and those dear to us coming after us, we must link up with those people and help our governments steer a better course than they collectively have been doing.

We've caught a glimpse of the abyss.

But we've also been shown the pathway to heaven, through love.

May each of us choose, carefully. Amen.

INSIDER-OUTSIDER

READING

"Grown-up Lessons for a Not-yet Grown-up Person"

Thinking back on my experience, I don't think I knew what I was getting into. I don't think I knew what I was taking on, or how much I was going to suffer. I stood up for what I knew was right, even though it made my life miserable for a while. It caused so many complications, and for a long period of time I had to stand on my own, with no one who could relate to me.

Kids, especially twelve-year-old girls, can be terribly cruel. And of the six of us, I was the one who first realized how much we were hurting people. Somehow, my small tight group of friends and I got the idea it would be fun to ruin a few peoples' lives. I had no idea at the time that I would be one of them. We did this by singling a person out and deliberately putting them down. However, I don't think any of us knew how cruel we were being.

I took part in being mean to my friend the first time, but the second time we tried to do it, I realized we were doing something wrong. I stood up for my friend and said, despite harsh looks, that I was friends with her and wasn't going to stop being her friend. But as fate would have it, we switched places. I was the dork, the loser, the odd man out, and for the first time I began to understand how much it hurt.

I think for the first part, I denied it. I wouldn't admit what was happening to me. I didn't want to see myself that way. Every time I tried to be me, they stepped on me. They used every opportunity they had to put me down. So finally, I began to believe all of the things they said. Everything I did was to try to please them. My self-esteem dropped so that I only had an ounce left, and I hated them for that. I hated them for hurting me over and over, and I hated them for not liking me. But at the same time all I wanted was to be their friend.

It's only now, a whole year after, that I'm beginning to understand all the lessons I learned from this experience.

I think the whole experience must have been confusing, upsetting, and so mind-blowing that I didn't understand. We all had this fear of not being a part of the group. And when we were kicked out of the group, we jumped at the thought of being friends with them again. I think it's because everyone wants to belong, to be a part of something; everyone likes to feel needed. It's so hard, sitting alone, watching others laugh and have a good time, and not being a part, that makes you want it even more.

After all of this, I feel as if the Golden Rule is a saying we should all live by. It makes so much sense, I understand it intellectually, and now, emotionally. But it was not until they turned the tables on me, until I was the victim, that I understood.

At this point in my life, the thing I always have to keep in my mind is: nobody's opinion of me should be more important than my opinion of myself.

I need to know that. I need to be comfortable with myself. And even if I have to remind myself of that over and over, I will because I know who I am.

—Sarah Flynn, age 14
April 19th Credo

SERMON
June 14, 1998

On April 19 past, our junior high students led both of our Sunday morning services as a culmination of their Affirmation Class this year, in which they were asked to write a short, and admittedly transitional, "credo" of what their most important personal beliefs were at this time in their lives.

A large part of each service was given to their delivery of their "credos." Because there were so many of them, nineteen in all, they had to be divided between the 10 a.m. and the 11:15 a.m. services.

Polly and I attended both services. I must tell you, we were almost spellbound by the experience. We wished that every person with even the faintest interest in All Souls could have been present to get an idea of what our twelve- to-fourteen-year-old youngsters are thinking.

These were young people seriously wrestling with ideas about God, about possible afterlife, reincarnation, good and evil, the relationship of the moral life to one's religious life.

Let me just give you an idea of the subjects that were touched that morning: there were references to Voltaire, Greek mythology, mathematical certainty vs. religious certainty, the meaning of the holocaust, stereotyping, whether it's possible to live without intolerance in a society riddled with intolerance, what it means to belong to a religion, why we feel a pang of remorse when we pass a beggar, even when we don't put a quarter in his or her cup, and why we cry in a movie like Schindler's List—even why Christmas has to be spelled with a "t"—why couldn't it be spelled with just one or two "s's"? A lot of issues were taken up.

Hearing our junior highs on April 19 rocked me back to the realization that young people of their age are almost fully formed adults, with the basic ideas and attitudes in place that will guide them the rest of their lives. Three weeks later our senior highs gave us a similarly remarkable presentation.

I know from my experiences with young people, particularly in three schools in New York City, that our young people grow up faster than we imagine possible. All we have to do is blink our eyes three times and say, "Where did the time go, anyway?" These same young people are moving into positions of leadership in our society, appearing in the newspapers, finding cures for ancient diseases, even preaching in our pulpits.

As I sat in the pew that morning, I had three inspirations, in rapid-fire order:

1. To use this morning's service, to which I was already committed, as an opportunity to respond to our nineteen junior highs,

2. To have one of our junior highs assist in the service today, reading a part of her statement of April 19, hence Sarah's appearance here this morning, and

3. To put a focus on the theme "Insider-Outsider," which I decided could be the basis of a sermon.

It struck me that while every participant was ready and willing to talk about "God," a few giving definitions, many more admitting to confusion, and a few readily admitting that they would probably be confused on the subject of God the rest of their lives, there was an underlying theme in all of their presentations that wasn't expressed openly, except by Sarah, who talked about what it feels like to be a junior high, wanting to fit into society, while at the same time maintaining one's own growing independence and individuality.

It's the sense of sometimes being on the inside, where the whole world is your oyster; you're accepted just as you are, the sky's the limit—and sometimes being on the outside, where you sense that nobody understands you, or will go to bat for you when the chips are down, or perhaps even be there in some disaster or at the end of your life when you've outlived everybody you care a lot about.

Hearing them took me back to my junior high days. It might be surprising to some of the junior highs here to know that a geezer seventy years old was once a junior high. Let me tell you what it was like for me to be a junior high.

One day, around the age of twelve, I rode my bike farther than I had ever ridden it, by far, out Northwestern Highway in Detroit, about seven miles I figured, until I was really in the country. I pulled off into a field with very tall grass, and first sat down, then lay down and listened to the sounds.

I remember hearing traffic on the highway a quarter mile away, and I remember the gentle swishing of the tall grass as the warm breeze blew through it. But I remember, even more, one bird singing, for a long time. I thought it might be a meadowlark. But what did I know about birds?!

But I did know something. There was not a happier sound on the planet that day than that one bird singing. I knew that I wouldn't leave while the bird continued to sing. And when it finally left I continued lying in the warm sun, feeling that I had entered a new stage of life. I hadn't heard of the philosopher Rene Descartes, who said, "I think, therefore I am," but I had my own version of his dictum: "I feel, therefore I am, I am one, I am one person, completely separated from every other person who was, is, or ever will be; I am one—with a universe, which contains many ones, including a bird which may have been contemplating its oneness even as I contemplated mine."

That's a junior high thought. Younger children don't think that way, they are too wrapped up in what their crowd is doing to want to lie in a field for an hour. But it comes to them too in time.

Let nobody think, if the memory of their youth is so blurred, that junior high isn't a very, very tough experience. It's tough with parents, it's tough with teachers, it's tough with their contemporaries. And all the time they have to be sorting out just what they want to do at the next stage, where high school looks like a dark, ominous cloud moving toward them.

I was in the seventh grade in Bagley School in Detroit one afternoon at 2 o'clock when our class changed teachers. That is, the class remained in their seats, while Miss Helen Cannon left and Mrs. Josephine Strauss came in. They met in the doorway. The class happened to be very quiet at the moment. Miss Cannon said to Mrs. Strauss, "Are you as sick and tired of that Dick Leonard as I am?" Mrs. Strauss replied without a moment's hesitation, "I certainly am!"

I was absolutely thunderstruck, not to say chagrined in front of the whole class. I guess it had never occurred to me that *anyone* could be sick and tired of *me*. And here were two people wishing apparently that I'd find another planet.

Did it hurt? You bet it did. It still hurts, or I wouldn't remember today, even the tones of their voices and how they looked, standing in the doorway.

Did it change me? Yes. I think it did. Up to that point I had thought of myself as a sort of classroom clown, trying to make everybody laugh. For the first time I saw myself as an irritant, easily done without. I quietly resolved that I would try harder to see things from the teachers' point of view.

Junior high can be cruel in terms of one's relationships to school buddies and especially to those of the opposite sex. I've told our "Stories with Soul" group several times about the rage and complete humiliation I felt when I saw my then girlfriend laughing with a new boyfriend, playing ping-pong, not knowing that I happened to be observing them. Up to that point ping-pong had been *our* game, and I had supposed only we were able to enjoy it that much. I was so angry at being displaced that I actually had trouble speaking for twenty-four hours.

Incidentally, it's that kind of anger, set in a culture where weapons are readily available to adults and children alike, that worries our educators and parents.

As Sarah captured in her credo, one day you're on the "inside," the next day you may be on the "outside." It is a mind-blowing experience to be on the outside when you want to be inside. If it's any consolation, young people, any adult here will tell you that it is an experience one doesn't outgrow. It happens to us adults probably as frequently as it does to you.

There was another event in my elementary school days that I've thought about often over the years, and I find it relates exactly to this morning's theme, "Insider-Outsider."

One day a new student showed up in our class. She was not much on looks. The teacher said, "I want to introduce you all to Iloo Friedberg." I didn't know what an appropriate response would be, sitting in my chair. Then, in the quiet, at least a half dozen of the students responded by booing.

I was probably not the only student who almost went through the floor, first with amazement, then with embarrassment for the poor young woman, who must at the moment have felt she stood completely alone and defenseless in a very hostile world.

You see, until then, living in a very homogenous Anglo-Saxon community, I didn't know what racial or religious bigotry was. I probably couldn't have defined the word *prejudice* if my life depended on it.

But some of the students knew. They knew that Iloo was different from the rest of us in several ways: she was new, she was dressed differently from us, and she was Jewish. They saw a chance to put themselves on the inside, and someone else on the outside.

I've often wondered what happened to Iloo. Was she able to live out the rest of her life in reasonable happiness? Or did that experience of feeling completely rejected by her new schoolmates linger and embitter her and possibly even greatly shorten her life? I wish, fifty-five years later, that I could offer a formal apology on behalf of those of us who sat on our hands that day while others booed a complete stranger.

I want to do a little test now on the congregation, the whole congregation, not just the junior highs who happen to be here. This is for everybody.

How many of you know what the letters *DWI* stand for? If so, just put up your hands. Look at that. Apparently everybody knows *DWI*. Okay tell me, what do the letters stand for? Say it. (Response: Driving while intoxicated.)

Okay, now again, just putting up your hands but not saying anything, how many of you know what the letters *DWB* stand for? Say it. (About four voices: Driving while black.)

Did you all hear it? Driving while black. You ever hear that? You've never heard that? It's a phrase that blacks know. It's been in the newspapers quite a bit lately. I don't remember hearing it on TV, but I hope it's been there too.

It refers to the fact that black drivers are much more apt to be pulled over to the side of the road by police than white drivers. And heaven forbid you are black and start to reach into your back pocket for identification—your chances of being shot at that moment are much higher than when I reach into my back pocket for identification.

I cannot talk about the subject of "Insider-Outsider" without talking about racism, because racism is out there. And it's in here, in every one of us, in all of us. In some places in the world race doesn't matter, but the United States is not one of them.

The Unitarian Universalist Association has wrestled with this problem long before I joined its ranks in 1959. It has to wrestle with the problem, because for all its espousal of democratic ideals and support of social action causes, the UUA membership nationwide remains today more than 95 percent white. We are somehow "turning off" many of the same people who could benefit *us* by making us more diverse in our points of view and experience.

Because we don't know why we turn off people whose insights we need, or blame them for not being enough like us, we reveal our own racism, our own smugness, our own willingness to play the "insider" to complete strangers on the outside.

The UUA's President's Council, which happens to include John Reidy, Polly, and me from this congregation, gave a long weekend in March to a training session in anti-racism. Blacks and whites led it, blacks and whites participated vigorously in it, and it was a cathartic experience for the fifty or so persons present. So much that they unanimously passed a strong resolution recommending that every church and fellowship subject itself to a similar kind of training session.

It's a tough exercise, make no mistake about it, helping everyone in a group share their strongest feelings about race and the role it plays unconsciously most of the time in our actions. But it is worth it. John, Polly, and I recommend it strongly for All Souls, hopefully sooner rather than later.

I had been in an anti-racism workshop before. And, as most of you know, I have given a fair share of my ministry to the civil rights struggle.

But one always learns a lot in free and open discussion, and I learned a lot in our President's Council workshop. I learned in a new way from people of another color how easy it is for me to walk in the streets of New York and go about my business while only being reminded a few times in the day, if at all, that my skin, by accident of birth, happens to be white—while my black brother or sister, perhaps my ministerial colleague, perhaps my artistic superior, is reminded all day long of his color by the constraints that a predominantly white culture places on a person of color.

My final words this morning are directed back to our junior highs.

Yes, the tensions of feeling yourself sometimes on the inside and sometimes on the outside are going to continue, right through the rest of your life. Sometimes you will find yourself a part of the team, and the team will win the game, and you will make the crucial score, and the whole world will be behind you, indeed will love you.

And sometimes you will find yourself where you do not feel particularly wanted, or you will find out how very, very hostile, even life-threatening, the world can be, and you will feel at that moment that you are absolutely alone; no one will help you.

Part of growing up is slowly realizing that things are neither that good, nor that bad. When your team wins, another team is perhaps desolate. Take time to put your arm round a loser's shoulder and cry a little bit with that person.

And when you are a loser (and we've all been there), remember that you are part of a community, many of whom have been where you are; many care, some will even be helpful, and you will not always be alone.

The "best," I have learned painfully, is always ahead. We keep coming out of cocoons into a newer undreamed-of life. I guess that's my version of reincarnation, which so many of you talked about.

Finally, it is our religious faith, our own individualized, patchwork, not quite coherent but nevertheless meaningful, religious faith that makes the difference and holds us together in tough times.

We adults wish our junior highs the best. We very openly admire and envy your youth.

And we thank all of our young people for enriching All Souls Church.

One Life

READING

"A Considerable Speck"

A speck that would have been beneath my sight
On any but a paper sheet so white
Set off across what I had written there.
And I had idly poised my pen in air
To stop it with a period of ink
When something strange about it made me think.
This was no dust speck by my breathing blown,
But unmistakably a living mite
With inclinations it could call its own.
It paused as with suspicion of my pen,
And then came racing wildly on again
To where my manuscript was not yet dry;
Then paused again and either drank or smelt—
With loathing, for again it turned to fly.
Plainly with an intelligence I dealt.
It seemed too tiny to have room for feet,
Yet must have had a set of them complete
To express how much it didn't want to die.
It ran with terror and cunning crept.
It faltered; I could see it hesitate;
Then in the middle of the open sheet
Cower down in desperation to accept
Whatever I accorded it of fate.

I have none of the tenderer-than-thou
Collective regimenting love
With which the modern world is being swept.
But this poor microscopic item now!
Since it was nothing I knew evil of
I let it lie there till I hope it slept.

I have a mind myself and recognize
Mind when I meet with it in any guise.
No one can know how glad I am to find
On any sheet the least display of mind.

—Robert Frost

SERMON
June 9, 1996

The inspiration for this morning's theme came out of a meeting Polly and I attended in early May. We are members, along with John Reidy of this congregation, of a group of Unitarian Universalists called the President's Council. John Buehrens, a former co-minister of this church, who was elected in 1993 to the presidency of the Unitarian Universalist Association, has put together a group of about fifty people to advise him on long-term policies for the association. The group meets two or three times a year.

In May we were in Salt Lake City. We found ourselves in a room with people many of whom we barely knew, if at all. This was the third President's Council Polly and I had attended, but we had to miss two council meetings recently, so we were about in the same boat as everyone else, not knowing many people there. You can appreciate that moment when council members sat at a number of tables, looking pretty mysterious and even awesome to one another.

The program person had a marvelous ice-breaker in store for us. She asked us to take turns coming to the microphone, and that each give three pieces of information: (1) our name, (2) something that would identify us, and then (3) some bit of information about ourselves that others in the room wouldn't know about.

The first person gave, as the unknown fact, that she played the dulcimer for her own amusement. The second person, that she enjoyed making pottery. Henry Groppe, co-chair of the meetings, allowed that he had milked 44,562 cows in his lifetime. Someone else was also an amateur potter. Someone else had not only milked cows but had ridden one once.

Another had proposed to his wife with a message on the sail of a big schooner. Yet another, and then another, and then another, turned out to be amateur potters. I suppose before the two days were over they had formed the Unitarian Universalist Clay Throwers Association. A woman who did not look particularly distinguished turned out to be a federal judge, and her secret was that she had been a classmate of Elizabeth Dole.

When my turn came I gave my name, my connection with All Souls, and then, grasping for something that nobody in the room could have possibly have known, reported that Polly and I had just returned from Bermuda, where I had played in a chess tournament and finished fourth.

Later, the minister of our church in Salt Lake City came up and asked me if I remembered him, Tom Goldsmith. I couldn't make the connection. He said, "I once won a half-gallon of root beer from you at the Homestead Camp!" The light went on. "Tommy Goldsmith! I remember you—you were about in the sixth grade then!" (In those days I gave a gallon of A&W root beer at the camp to anyone who beat me at chess, and a half-gallon to anyone who got a draw from me. I managed to lose two or three gallons of root beer over the summer. Tommy Goldsmith had once gotten a draw, and we both remembered it all too well.)

The amazing playout of this little drama was that the Rev. Tom Goldsmith, now a Unitarian Universalist minister of our largest church in Utah, had passed on his love of chess to his son, and his son has just become the Utah State Junior Chess Champion!

The reason I've gone at some length into the variety of "secrets" the various Council members divulged, is that it was becoming increasingly apparent, as each got up in his or her turn, that we were an exceedingly interesting group of people. All reserve between us evaporated in that little exercise; we hunted each other out to compare notes on our hobbies and our professions and our geographical backgrounds.

In fact, it inspired me to an even more important thought, at least important to me, and that is that any person whom you see, no matter how uninteresting that person might seem to appear, if you could get that person talking about his or her idiosyncrasies, he or she would prove to be of unlimited interest to you.

Hence the title of this morning's sermon: "One Life." Every *one life*, yours, mine, the (to us) nameless person on the street, is in fact, an incredibly interesting person, if their story be told. Too bad we don't take time to learn the small things about each other and the people we rub shoulders with, to learn the few degrees of separation that actually exist between us and the rest of humankind.

Not only is each one of us an incredibly complex and interesting individual from a psychological point of view, how can we begin to describe our complexity from a physiological point of view!

Zoology was not my best subject in college. In fact I took it as a required science course, thinking it dealt with the animals in the zoo, and was surprised that we never left the study of the workings of the human body. But somewhere in that course it dawned on me that there is nothing more amazing than how a human egg is fertilized, how it subdivides, and continues to subdivide, with cells specializing to become parts of nerves and eyes and feet, so that eventually a simply functioning human is as complicated as anything in the universe, including the very stars in their relationships with each other.

When Gary Kasparov defeated the Deep Blue IBM chess computer in February, 1996, he was defeating a machine that could look at a million chess combinations every second and weigh them against each other, and Kasparov still won. He struck a blow, not only for himself and for chess, but even more for you and me. After all, we have brains just like Kasparov's, not tuned as acutely as his to chess, but perhaps tuned more acutely in other areas.

In other words, in just walking down the street from 79th Street to 78th Street, each one of us apparently processes millions of bits of information almost simultaneously, the way the strongest computer does. It's good to remember that each of us is a miracle physiologically, as well as in our personalities.

For me, the horror of war is that even one such unbelievable part of creation is deliberately destroyed by another, not to mention the millions in a holocaust. *EVEN ONE!* That's the horror.

Pictures of mass graves, for example, as we saw in World War II, or more recently in Cambodia and Bosnia, create a kind of ultimate sadness in me, because I know that every victim was at one time a beautiful, marvelously functioning individual, at the pinnacle of God's creation if you will, loving and beloved, able to dance and write poetry and make people laugh, and to ease someone else's problems.

I feel the same way when I go into a hospital and see someone who may barely be functioning anymore. I see such people as they were, beautiful children full of promise, or accomplished adults.

And the man and woman begging on the street! In all likelihood they are disease-ridden. For a brief instant I see them as they were, free of worry, optimistic about the future, lovers of many of the same things we love, real humans. Even in their illness, they are miracles of creation, functioning universes of cells and nerve endings and synapses and drives. I want to help such a person. A part of me says, "Give them everything!" And another part of me says, "Give them what you think they need," like dignity in your mind, support of programs that will feed and house them, and a voice at the voting booth on their behalf, or even a loan to help them turn things around.

So while I go around having to fight the sadness from seeing people living at a low level of their potential, any flagging of my spirit is remedied just by observing the world around us and the animate world in particular.

Polly and I love to travel, as most of you know. We are continually reminded of how vast the world is, and how much we are all controlled by the world, rather than the other way around.

When we were in Africa this past January we had one eye-popping or mind-blowing experience after another. In Kenya, the lions were mating. We happened to be there in the mating period, which, for a pair of lions, is only about three days long. And we learned something that they don't tell you, in children's books anyway. That is that two lions will mate every fifteen minutes for three days. We came upon more than one "honeymooning" pair, and sure enough, within fifteen minutes they were mating for the um-teenth time. Eventually that male goes off to live by himself, and another male that has been hanging around the edges of the activity, comes to relate to the female and her eventual cubs. (Don't ask me why lions have this arrangement. It is just a part of nature.)

In fact, not only did the lions mate for us, so did most of the other animals: zebras, giant tortoises, cattle, birds, even butterflies. We began to wonder if there something about us that made the animals amorous.

We saw every major animal on this trip except a leopard (and one of those almost came into our car in 1983). I found the insects to be just as interesting as the elephants, rhinos, giraffes, cheetahs, and the five-foot-long sleeping boa constrictor we happened on. We saw spiders of all sizes and shapes, and Polly found a baby scorpion walking across the table one night at dinner. (What do you do with a baby scorpion? We let it go).

We observed several instances of dung beetles at work. If you are not fully aware of the habits of the dung beetle, let me give you the basics. The male and female find the spot where they are going to build their nest. Then they go off together to find a suitable piece of dung left by another animal. They shape it into a ball. Then the female jumps aboard for the ride while the male rolls the ball toward the nest.

To roll it, he has to get on the back end of the ball, put his head and front legs down toward the path, and push with back legs while he is upside down. But he can't see where he is going, so after he has rolled it a foot or so, he climbs up on top of the ball to make sure of his direction, then goes head down behind again, to push some more.

The female keeps out of the way of all this effort, by implanting herself on the side of the ball, and just going around and around while the male alternately pushes and then climbs up to see how he is doing. When they get to the selected spot, the male rolls the ball into the hole they have made for it, the female lays the eggs, and then she does a lot of the work of raising their family. We got some great photos of males rolling dung balls while the females rode free, going around and around and around.

While I don't get soupy about not taking any life under any circumstances (including a baby scorpion's), it is a miracle that insects can be so purposeful. Or that giant tortoises, living for 400 years, and dating back to a period before the dinosaurs 200 million years ago, have for these hundreds of millions of years gotten by with brains the size of one's thumbnail.

As Forrest and Galen have said many times from this pulpit, the greatest miracle, in fact the only miracle when you think about it, is life itself. To participate in it at all, is to be given the greatest gift that we could possibly ask for, and alongside which all other gifts lose their importance.

When things get tough, and every one of us has had unbearable experiences at one time or another and can conceivably be going through one now, when things get tough, the way out is by keeping some kind of perspective on what we have been given, and to nurture life, if only with a walk in the park and observing an insect hard about its business.

Every *one life* participates in a process that the most devoted scientist can only begin to understand, but which all of us can appreciate and feel grateful for. Whether you call it Oversoul, as Emerson did, or the Elan Vital, as did Henri Bergson, or the Prime Mover of Aristotle, or the Hindu Karma, or Eternal Life, as did Jesus, we are caught up in a single event that makes us family with each other, and with the animal kingdom, and with the universe itself.

Let us resolve to make the most of it.

A View From the Bottom

READING

The Lord answered Job from the whirlwind, saying,
"Where were you when I laid the foundations of the earth?
Declare, if you have insight.
Upon what were its bases sunk, or who laid
    its corner stone?
Who enclosed the sea with doors and established its barrier
And said 'Thus far shall you come and no farther,
And here shall your proud waves be stayed'?

Have you gone to the sources of the sea,
Or walked in the hollows of the deep?
Have the gates of death been revealed to you,
Or can you see the gates of darkness?
Have you considered the breadth of the earth?
Tell, if you know all this.

Have you been to the storehouses of snow,
Or do you see the storehouses of hail,
Which I have reserved against the time of distress?
From whose womb did the ice come forth?
And who gave birth to the hoarfrost of the skies,
When the waters congeal like stone,
And the surface of the deep is frozen solid?"

Then Job replied to the Lord, saying;
"Behold, I am insignificant; what can I answer thee?
I put my hand over my mouth.
I have spoken once, and I will not reply;
Yes, twice; but not again."

—Book of Job, Chapters 38-40

SERMON
April 24, 1994

When Polly and I returned from our trip to Antarctica in January of this year, a number of church members said to me, "You *must* tell us about your experiences in a sermon, so the whole congregation can hear about it."

At the same time I had misgivings, because one thing a sermon shouldn't be is a travelogue. Several times in the past on a Sunday morning I've run on about some place we've seen.

In fact I was really brought up short when a church member who has been to the Antarctic, and loved it, said to me, "But what could you possibly say that would be related to a Sunday morning church service?" It took some wind out of my sails.

Then another interesting thing happened. I called on a church member whose health has been poor, and who is in constant pain. I wondered what I could say to her that could help her in her duress. And before I could say anything she said, "I want you to tell me everything you can about your trip to Antarctica." An hour later I was still fielding one sharp question after another about life at the bottom of the earth. In opening a new world to her, I realized I had brought her pleasure, and hope and another measure of life.

Oliver Wendell Holmes said, "A mind that has been stretched by new experiences cannot go back to its old dimensions."

Just as Polly and I have been stretched by every trip we have taken, this sermon is offered in that spirit, that each of you, whatever your problems or achievements, will be stretched a bit by hearing of our adventure and have your view of the world subtly reshaped, as was ours.

The outstanding fact for us is that there is an immense area of the world, as big as Siberia and far larger than the United States, that has not been seen by 99.9999 percent of the people who have lived on earth since the beginning of time. It is an area that is almost completely inhospitable to human life during most of the months of the year. Fifty year-round stations now dot the continent, maintained by a number of countries. But they are lost in the size of Antarctica. It is as if every state in the United States had one square mile where people lived and the rest of the each state was barren and uninhabited by humans.

How can one convey the size of Antarctica? Perhaps by saying that the largest iceberg on record broke off from the Ross Ice Cap and was itself the size of the state of Rhode Island.

What once was a small, white, amorphous nothing at the bottom of conventional maps when I was growing up, is now seen to be an immense continent containing seventy percent of all the fresh water in the world.

So a view from the bottom of the earth changes the scale of everything happening above it. Of course we saw only a small part of it, three landings on the Palmer Peninsula, which reaches up toward Chile from where our ship, the Marco Polo, sailed.

The view from the bottom also reveals, at least in that area, a world of peace, an immense continent not contested by the countries of the world. Conflict could develop over minerals, oil and fishing rights, but so far the countries have determined that peaceful methods will be used to preserve one of the world's great wonders and blessings.

Long before the Cold War ended, and in spite of overlapping claims of nations in Antarctica, the assumption spread easily that everyone would benefit from preserving the integrity and the beauty of the continent by international agreements.

The longer I am a clergyperson, the more certain I am that reverence for life, to which the scriptures of many religions exhort us, means reverence for life on this planet earth, and the more I think that ecology and theology are intertwined. One cannot have a "love of life" and a disdain for how the world's resources are managed.

The very thought of sailing a big ship into Antarctica seems the antithesis of ecologically correct living, and concerned us deeply, even years ago, when we thought about such a trip. (As an aside let me say that Polly and I try hard in many ways to be good ecological citizens, such as not keeping a car, sorting our garbage, and not being wasteful with food. But a trip to the Antarctic?)

It looked plausible to us several years ago when it was announced that a ship would enter the Antarctic and come out without leaving a trace that it had been there. But before we could get on it, that ship was commandeered by a scientific organization, and has not been used by the general public.

Then along came the refitted Marco Polo, also advertising that it was ecologically sound, entering and leaving Antarctica without leaving a trace that it had been there. Sir Edmund Hillary, of Mount Everest fame, and other lecturers would highlight the environmental aspect of the trip.

We were convinced that this was our trip when we learned that the scientists who have been in Antarctica for many, many years had been very careless about their polluting tendencies, leaving oil drums everywhere, not to mention other toxic wastes. It had been tourists, in some cases politicians, who had seen the ecological mismanagement by the scientists, who had called for the first laws that had led to some cleaning up of scientific stations.

We signed on, thinking of ourselves as environmental pioneers, as well as fulfilling a long ambition that began at the Bronx Zoo in 1968. We passengers would make landings, but return without any damage to the wildlife or the environment, the same way Polly and I had visited the Galapagos Islands in 1985.

Actually, the ultimate test of my sincerity about environmentalism came while we were visiting the gentou penguin colony at Port Lockroy. Penguins are found in great numbers in Antarctica, but mostly around the edges of the continent. Except for emperor penguins, who hang around the South Pole, far inland, the others need the rock edges on which to nest. They migrate to other places during the colder months.

But one sees thousands of them at a time in January (which is summer down there, of course). In one rookery it was estimated that we were viewing 100,000 Adelie penguins at once on a hillside.

Our guides pointed out in advance that penguins are not housebroken. In fact, they spray whenever and wherever they like, often on each other, which is one reason for wearing boots and rubberized pants. The heavy clothing also provides protection from the weather and allows one to wade ashore from the rubber Zodiac boats that the ship carries.

If one walks to within fifteen feet of the penguins, which is as close as we were supposed to go, one is walking in a slippery excremental slime, made worse by melting snow and the jagged rocks. Falling down in the slime is particularly stressful.

That afternoon in Port Lockroy I not-so-cleverly dropped the notes I was writing into the gook. The pad came up quite dirty. All the pages were somewhat salvageable, except one. The temptation to tear that one empty page off and grind it into the snow was overwhelming.

But I thought about the basic premise of the trip, that we would not leave a trace behind, and as nonchalantly as possible I stuffed the smelly page into the side pocket of my parka for disposal later on the boat.

We found out, through lecture and experience, that the environment is more complex and brittle, particularly in the Southern Hemisphere, than we had imagined.

As important as the destruction of rain forests is elsewhere, or the development of acid rain or the accumulation of toxic wastes, the most ominous environmental problem for governments and scientists today is the depletion of the ozone layer. We wore heavy sunblock during all our outings, and still came back with a heavy tan, probably from the winds of up to a hundred miles per hour that we experienced on the ship.

But the bigger danger from ozone depletion is the possibility that krill, the almost invisibly small shrimp-like organisms that feed the world's food chain in the sea and swarm out only from under the Antarctic icecap in numbers of a billion to a swarm, may become sterile under the ozone hole and stop breeding, which would effectively end life in the big oceans.

Whales, by the way, swim through the ocean with their mouths open, gulping and processing billions of krill every hour. If you want to think about the interdependent web of all life, take into account the fact that while whales at one time were being severely reduced through hunting, there was a lot more krill in the water. The penguin population multiplied many times over in that period. Now that some species of whales, at least, are making a comeback, it is bad news for the penguins, who will have less krill to feed on.

Another environmental surprise for us was the matter of the icecap itself, the depth of which averages two miles over the whole continent. (Even with New York's past severe winter, it is difficult to imagine ice as deep as from 80th to 42nd St.)

In fact, the ice has been there so long, compacting from the ice above it, that it has become rock. Only as it slowly moves eventually to the sea, over several hundred thousand years, does it melt and return to water.

And this was a surprise: scientists now believe that two miles under the ice are active volcanoes, like the one at sea level on Deception Island that threatens to erupt any day. But other volcanoes are two miles down, and their eruptions do not disturb the icecap.

We passed Deception Island at two in the morning. The scientific station there had been abandoned. I confess relief that we had successfully skirted its volcano. (More recently we were within sight of the Arenal Volcano in Costa Rica. Five times within two and a half hours we heard the full-throated rumble of that volcano and saw hot stones landing on the hillside. Costa Rica alone has five active volcanoes. Any one of them can put the "fear of God" or the "respect for mother nature" into a person by its roaring alone.)

The third area where we thought we learned so much was in the area of plate tectonics. In addition to Sir Edmund Hillary, we happened to have aboard as lecturer a geologist, Giles Allard, voted the outstanding lecturer at the University of Georgia for seventeen consecutive years.

In almost daily lectures he demonstrated how the plates that underlie the continents move, how Antarctica was once much larger, embracing Africa, South America and Australia, and even India, and how scientists know today beyond a shadow of a doubt how and when it broke apart. Antarctica was once about where the Sahara Desert is today. We were bombarded with facts that remind us that our planet is still evolving and shifting and changing. One of his lectures concluded, "We know that Los Angeles will one day be up alongside San Francisco, but that is some time away, a few million years."

I didn't want this to be a travelogue. I've omitted descriptions of our crossing the Drake Passage in rough seas between South America and Antarctica; descriptions of the five species of penguins we encountered, or anything about the birds; the fun of being near the nesting albatrosses, with their six-foot wing span; or anything about Buenos Aires, Iguassu Falls, or Rio de Janeiro, where we ended our trip.

What I've tried to do, rather, is let you know that Polly and I have had a mind-blowing (Oliver Wendell Holmes expressed it as "mind-stretching") experience, that has left us with a slightly different outlook than before.

With Job, in today's reading, we have asked where the storehouses of snow are, from whose womb the ice came, and who or what made the waters congeal like stone.

I assure you that a "View from the Bottom" is sometimes a pretty good vantage point for appreciating this incredible world that surrounds us.

May the joy of discovery, of people and places, and simply being alive in a world beyond our imagining, be with us each day that we are given.

One Leg at a Time

READING

And upon the first day of the week, when the disciples came together to break bread, Paul preached unto them, ready to depart on the morrow, and continued his speech until midnight.

And there were many lights in the upper chamber, where they were gathered together.

And there sat in a window a certain young man named Eutychus, being fallen into a deep sleep; and as Paul was long preaching, he sunk down with sleep, and fell down from the third loft, and was taken up dead.

And Paul went down, and fell on him, and embracing him said, "Trouble not yourselves; for his life is in him."

When he therefore was come up again, and had broken bread, and eaten and talked a long while, even till break of day, so he departed.

And they brought the young man alive and were not a little comforted.

—Book of Acts XX, 7-12

SERMON
August 9, 1992

Sometime next month, if I play my cards right and don't step in front of a bicyclist going the wrong way on Lexington Avenue, I expect to turn age sixty-five. Polly thinks that I have been making too much of that in public these days, and that sooner or later somebody's going to drop a discrete hint that many people think of retiring at sixty-five!

As a matter of fact, I've thought of retiring at sixty-five, if not next month, perhaps in one of the succeeding eleven months.

But I've also thought a lot about not retiring. I've had fantasies of coming across the park at age eighty-five several days a week, several months a year, to pretend I was doing useful work. And at age ninety, standing before a wedding couple whose names I can't remember at the critical moment, trying to pronounce them husband and wife.

Some of you know, and John and Forrest surely know, that I find that preaching a sermon is one of the hardest things I do—or not preaching it exactly, but preparing it. I take a long time to prepare a sermon, and an even longer time worrying about the fact that I will have to prepare one. The preaching is not so bad. I like, and am used to, getting up in front of people and hearing my words flow, sometimes smoothly, sometimes haltingly. The thought of the responsibility that I may have a hundred, two hundred, five hundred people in front of me who have come specifically for guidance, a few in deep depression, perhaps one toying with suicide, that's an overwhelming thought that almost stops me dead in my tracks.

What can one say in a sermon or in a prayer, perhaps only one thought, that will keep a door open, maybe give a number of people a new slant on life that makes a difference for them in the weeks ahead, and for those who feel their lives are well-ordered and "working nicely, thank you," not bore the bejabbers out of them?

One of our Unitarian Universalist ministers wrote recently that while sermons "came" to his fellow clergy, he had to really go out and look for his. I'm surely in his group. I'm already deeply aware that I've agreed to lead the service here on November 8, only three months way, while Forrest and John couldn't tell you how many times they'll go through the same motions between now and then.

Even when I preached every Sunday, as I did in my first church in East Rockaway and later for about ten years in the Flatbush UU

Church, getting ready for each Sunday was a little like pushing the rock uphill for seven days only to have it roll back.

Why would one do it?

Well, because people would tell you on the way out that they had enjoyed your sermon. But more importantly because, for one or two people each week, you could see that it really had made a difference.

It was just in thinking about my difficulties in preparing services that I was driven to this morning's topic "One Leg at a Time." The gist of that may be a mystery to some of you, but others already undoubtedly have this sermon figured out.

It struck me that perhaps one of the most important things I can say to you, and that we can say to each other, is that we are all very, very human beings, whether we are in positions of leadership, or we are looking to others for leadership, whether we are in the pulpit, conducting business, trying to work things out in our families or whatever. All of us are very human. We fall asleep and topple out of the window when we might be hearing important words, like Eutychus in the Book of Acts. We are taken up for dead only to somehow live again.

I'm sure that almost every day George Bush gets up, goes to the mirror in the bathroom, looks at the stubble on his face and the darkening eyes and lines etched more deeply each month and says to himself at least, "My God! Is this the president of the United States?"

And then he puts on his pants, as the old expression goes, "one leg at a time."

We all have dozens of stories, if not hundreds, about people we have seen in a highly exalted light, whom an event makes us see quite differently.

At one of the weddings I did at the United Nations I knew in advance that the best man would be Dr. Michael Debaky, the famous heart surgeon from Houston. I was a little concerned about meeting a person of such stature.

Much to my surprise, I found him to be about the most nervous best man I had ever run into, to the point that I finally said to him,

"Is this really harder for you than doing a heart transplant?" He answered, "You'd better believe it," and I imagined I could see his hands shaking. I was tempted to say, "If I ever need a heart transplant, I'll think twice before I have you do it," but of course I didn't say that.

At another of my weddings, Yo Yo Ma, the premier cellist in the world today in most people's estimation, was to perform in the middle of the ceremony. I was more than amazed before the wedding to see him run down a flight of stairs, two stairs at a time, with his priceless instrument gripped in one hand. It didn't prevent him from playing like a magician when his moment came, but I felt I had been privileged to see a very human side of a personality that radiates unbounded energy in all directions. But he too, I dare say, puts on his pants one leg at a time, and perhaps has moments, even periods, of uncertainty about himself.

Let me expand this a moment into the area of religion, and say that we all have a tendency to want to create infallible gods that we can model ourselves after, and even worship.

On Wednesday nights we've been having a series of adult education classes using eight taped lectures on religion given by the headmaster of the Hotchkiss School, Dr. Robert Oden.

He makes an interesting point that the relationship between the Divine Being, or God, and the human being is fuzzy in all religions. In fact, "God" and the great human leader of a people are really quite interchangeable. Jesus "becomes" God in Christianity; Buddha performs miracles even though he himself makes no reference to God; the pharaoh is seen as divine by those who succeed him, even though scholarship today believes that he did not see himself as God-king, as we learned in elementary school, even in building the pyramids. The pope speaks to the faithful and is seen to be infallible in matters of faith.

We elevate extraordinary humans to the role of God and then are let down hard when they reveal their humanity.

I don't need to remind you that Jesus continually called attention to his humanity even as people tried to make him the Messiah or Son of God.

Another interesting point that professor Oden makes is that the East, the Middle East, India, and China, which we like to think of as mystical and hardly capable of being understood by our so-called western analytical minds, is not nearly as mystical as we would like to believe and no more mystical than we are, to them and to ourselves.

Professor Oden's area of expertise is in the language of Sumeria, that area between the Tigris and the Euphrates that probably gave rise to the first civilization. That language, Sumerian, is not related to any other known language and served a complicated society that existed from 3400 B.C.E. to about 2000 B.C.E.

He tells us that once one is "inside the language," so to speak, one finds people doing, acting, and saying what one would expect them to be doing at their level of development. People are not different basically from one culture to another.

Let me give you an example out of personal experience. In May of 1988, Polly and I were in about the most exotic place we have visited, Outer Mongolia, between China and Siberia.

We had taken the train down to Ulan Bator from Lake Baikal and then two flights into the Gobi Desert to live several nights each in two yurt camps. (Yurts are those marvelous round tents with the chimney up the middle that proved so comfortable, and which are moved continually around the countryside. Each tent can be broken down in about an hour, and it and all of its furnishings can be transported on the backs of four camels.) We felt a long way from Times Square in our yurt.

One of our trips took us to a Buddhist monastery that was built in 1838. For a long time under Communist rule, temples were closed and the monks were dispersed or were killed. However, by 1988 the tide had turned and this monastery now housed two hundred monks.

We stepped into the main temple, and it was like stepping back five hundred years in a time machine. It was packed with monks in orange, mostly quite old men, perhaps a hundred of them, chanting the chants over and over. They sat facing the center, in rectangular configurations several rows deep.

Visitors could just barely squeeze in and work their way around to the very back, which we were permitted to do.

Meanwhile, as they chanted, the monks were being continuously served bowls of something I presumed to be rice, as needed, from dispensers in two corners of the room. The room was laden from top to bottom with gold and brightly colored objects, Buddha statues, drums, candles, other musical instruments.

The impression we got was that the chants had been going forever and would continue to go on forever.

As they sang, most of the monks glanced at the sacred texts of the chants, unrolled in their laps, which would be rolled up again in cloth at the end; others knew the chants by heart.

The chants did have beginnings and ends. At the end of each, the singsong trailed off with lower notes, and then started again immediately. Wouldn't we have liked to have been able to tape that sound of a hundred male voices!

We slowly worked our way around the back toward the empty Dalai Lama's throne. As we stopped momentarily, we saw two old monks in the back row. One glanced around at me, nudged his friend in the middle of the chant. They both looked at me, but it was not at me they were looking. The first one had spotted a small Rubik's Cube dangling from my belt, a cube that I wore on several trips to the Far East.

They grinned from ear to ear, and we all exchanged looks that carried a ton of information in almost the twinkling of an eye.

In a single glance his eyes said to me, "I know Rubik's Cubes. We don't speak the same language, but I would love to see you demonstrate it and talk about the mathematics of it and teach me how to do it. It would be a better use of my time than chanting the same things over and over again." (Well, maybe his look didn't quite say all of that.) I hope he read into my glance that if language and time commitments were not a factor, I would be delighted not only to teach him about Rubik's Cubes but also learn and think about the chants that took up about eight hours of their every day.

"The East is not as mysterious as we make it out to be!" The words of Professor Oden ring true in my head.

How many stories do we know about people who think they have almost nothing in common discovering that they have almost everything in common. They begin to discover it when they share a small piece of their humanity, like, "I had to have an operation on a trick finger too." Or, "My father also sold insurance." Or, "The last time I remember hearing that song was my mother singing it in the kitchen."

For all the hype that goes into making Michael Jordan "Air Jordan," or Margaret Thatcher "The Iron Lady," any cultural idol will confess that most of the person's energy goes into doing the most mundane, repetitious things imaginable at least ninety percent of the time. For the professional athlete, how much time has gone into simply lacing up sneakers or practicing hook shots all alone in a gymnasium, watching half of them go in and half of them fall out, and trying to move the percentages a few more points in his or her favor! How much time goes into packing and unpacking suitcases and sitting on buses, if one is fortunate enough to be on a team that has a schedule to keep!

One of Polly's nephews, Rick, is a "roadie." How many in this room know what a roadie is? (I was willing to bet not as many as ten!)

A roadie is responsible for moving all of the equipment of, say, a band of musicians from one engagement to the next, usually in a huge van, often at night, probably over a long distance, and getting them all set up electronically at their next stop so that they only have to walk on the stage and perform. Often it's a "one night stand," and everything has to be put away after the performance, and another long night of driving is undertaken.

A good roadie, by the way, makes good money, or he'd probably do something else.

There isn't a job that doesn't require just plain hard effort most of the time. Ask Bill Clinton and Al Gore, who must have gotten pretty tired of the bus they've been scooting around in.

Somehow the winners in life, whether it's in the Olympics, in politics, or just surviving spiritually in a world full of crushing forces, are the people who can plod with great difficulty by taking one step at a time.

This past week I visited in the hospital a young Unitarian Universalist woman from Tennessee who had come to New York to help a friend move. As a matter of fact, she had just been elected vice president of her Unitarian congregation in Memphis.

Before she could help her friend, however, she was stricken with unbearable pains, was rushed to Bellevue, and in twelve hours was diagnosed as having leukemia. Most of her time from that moment on had been spent crying, as she prepared for her return to Memphis and entering a hospital there for chemotherapy.

We visited for close to an hour. She put the question very bluntly: "Mr. Leonard, what do you tell somebody in my situation who has assumed she had a long life ahead and finds out that there may be very little time left?"

I tried to be completely honest. I said, "In a sense my advice is cheap because I have not been in that situation myself, nor had it happen to a close member of my family.

"But over the years, as a minister, I have talked with a number of people who have gotten terrific jolts—not only in terms of their health, but in such things as having a good job suddenly cut away, along with a sense of financial security, or suffered the accidental death of a child or some other complete disaster.

"And many of them have been able to tell me that they were able to get a different picture of life—that they are forced to live one day at a time. They stop to smell the roses, so to speak. They compare all the things they have taken for granted over the years with the extreme hardship that they see in other lives and in other parts of the world. They feel themselves become more human, and more appreciative of the process of which they are a part. And they do it somehow, doing the things each day that, while difficult, have to be done, and can be done with a level of satisfaction."

She wanted to talk about prayer and her longtime feeling that praying to a deity was medieval, and especially that praying for herself was selfish hypocrisy.

I told her that even having hopes for oneself or others is a form of prayer, so we're all engaged in prayer in some form, whether we know it or not. And that there was nothing wrong in praying for long life, that it was my prayer for her as well as for myself, among other prayers.

She has returned to Memphis, and I have telephoned her in the hospital room there, which surprised her.

But it also dawned on me that what she needed, more than anything else in a strange city, was just some evidence that somebody cared.

As Kenneth Patton said, "What more can we give to one another than our love and understanding?"

Sometimes I finish scanning a newspaper and it seems as though the world's problems are just too enormous for humanity to work out. Then I think of all the people in the world who would like to see wars ended, and starvation eliminated, and ignorance overcome, and disease successfully fought, all of them doing one thing at a time as they know best. And I have to believe that the reservoir of goodwill and caring is quite possibly enough to slowly bring a quality of life to our planet that we haven't enjoyed before.

I may be wrong in my judgment of the human potential, but I intend to keep on plodding, at age sixty-five, one leg or one day at a time, and my prayer is that you will find it possible, also, to smell the roses.

IN THE NAME OF ALLAH

READING

For Muslims at the turn of the century, the problem was inescapable. Islam was what was deepest in them. If to live in the modern world demanded changes in their ways of organizing society, they must try to make them while remaining true to themselves; and this would be possible only if Islam was interpreted to make it compatible with survival, strength and progress in the world. This was the starting-point of those who can be called "Islamic modernists." Islam, they believed, was not only compatible with reason, progress and social solidarity, the bases of modern civilization; if properly interpreted, it positively enjoined them. Such ideas were put forward by Jamal al-Din al-Afghani (1839–1897), an Iranian whose writings were obscure but whose personal influence was considerable and far flung. They were developed more fully and clearly in the writings of an Egyptian, Muhammad 'Abduh (1849–1905), whose writings were to have a great and lasting influence throughout the Muslim world. The purpose of his life, as he stated it, was: "to liberate thought from the shackles of imitation and understand religion as it was understood by the community before dissension appeared; to return, in the acquisition of religious knowledge, to its first sources, and to weigh them in the scale of human reason, which God has created in order to prevent excess or adulteration in religion, so that God's wisdom may be fulfilled and the order of the human world preserved; and to prove that, seen in this light, religion must be accounted a friend to science, pushing us to investigate the secrets of existence, summoning us to respect established truths and to depend on them in our moral life and conduct."

—From Albert Hourani's book
A History of the Arab Peoples

SERMON
April 14, 1991

On February 20 of this year the liberal theologians Harvey Cox and Forrest Church engaged in conversation before our congregation.

If you recall, we had just begun a full-scale bombing of Iraq. The world wondered where hostilities would take it. Harvey and Forrest together explored Christian-Jewish-Islamic relations in a memorable discussion.

Harvey made a strong point. He felt that we in the United States have practically cultivated a disdain and an ignorance of Islam over generations. The result is that we are almost inept in the Muslim world, and try to compensate by throwing our weight around. It is not the road for building a lasting peace.

I took their words seriously that night and began to take inventory of my experiences with Islam and of ways that I could begin to plug some pretty big areas of ignorance.

I thought back to my few courses in college and seminary in comparative religion. I think I learned a lot in those classes, but I also think I forgot a great deal.

I thought also of my experience in Bay Ridge, Brooklyn. Union Church was made up of both Syrians and Scandinavians. We had Abouchars and Sahadis and Haddads and Khourys. We also had Johnsons and Olsens and Johanssons and Swensens. If you were in that church you were either darker or you were lighter. And everyone got along exceedingly well.

But it dawned on me that all these Syrians were Presbyterian, or if they weren't Presbyterian, they were Syrian Orthodox and went to the Syrian Orthodox church across the street. I doubt that I met a single Muslim in Bay Ridge.

Community Church in Manhattan brought me my first real experience with diversity. I was the minister of education there for nine years and I did some catching up. One day I invited a Muslim speaker to come to the children's chapel. We agreed he would be there thirty minutes early so that we could test out what we might say in front of children.

To my dismay, he arrived at 11 a.m. instead of 10:30 a.m., and there I was with a perfect stranger in front of many children.

After welcoming him, I broke the ice with all I could think to say at the moment, something like, "There is a lot I don't know about Islam, but my impression of people who are Muslim is that they are very devout, that they believe very strongly what they believe, and, you know, there's not too much room for a nonbeliever in Islam to argue with them."

He smiled and said, "This tends to be true in all religions. The great prophet comes along, be he Jesus or Mohammed or Buddha, who has a vision for the whole of humanity. He wants to see people living in peace. Then the prophet dies and the followers begin to argue among themselves as to the correct interpretation of the leader's words. They say, 'I understand, but this person over there doesn't understand,' and divisions occur, and even hostility. The only recourse is to get back as much as possible to the original vision."

He was such a reasonable fellow that I found myself wishing I could be as reasonable in my approach to religion as he was.

I thought of a wedding I had had in St. Paul's Chapel at Columbia University. The groom's name was Hafizzula Bakban, the bride, Marcia Moses. He was Egyptian and a Muslim; she was American and Jewish. They were married in an Episcopal church by a Unitarian minister, so that they could live in Afghanistan, where he would teach English.

Think about that awhile, in terms of the power of love to conquer all complexity.

More recently I performed a wedding at the United Nations Chapel of a Shiite Muslim, a fellow in the diplomatic field, marrying a Jewish girl. Because his family was in Iran and were Shiites, she had gone to live with them for three months. She wore the chador and participated as fully as she could in their family life.

The family was so taken with this girl that they said to their son, "If you don't hurry up and marry this woman, you are going to lose her." This was in spite of any feeling they had about Zionism or whatever. They loved this girl.

They did in fact get married, and I thought, "This has got to be an example for all people, that whatever animosities are in the world, people can break through. Love can prevail."

My wife and I made two trips to North Africa, one in 1981 and one in 1984. We got a taste of Egypt, Jordan, and Morocco. I guess the Moroccan experience was the most outstanding, because we were there during Ramadan, the high holy month in Islam when people fast. They don't eat anything during the daylight hours, but they do eat and often carouse at night.

The consequence is that they tend to sleep during the day and also to be very, very restless during the day. We saw many fist fights in Morocco. Those we attributed to the fact that people were celebrating Ramadan and they just weren't used to those schedules. It was hot, and they wanted something to eat during the day. So instead of eating, they tended to get scrappy with one another. It was an experience for us that surprised us.

One experience at All Souls also surprised us. A young man died in an accident in 1986. He was an Iranian American. He had gone to a New Year's party in Greenwich Village. A good Muslim is not supposed to drink alcohol. The accident happened before anybody had even thought about breaking out alcohol. He leaned against the elevator door in the loft, the door gave way, he fell down the elevator shaft and was killed. He was an only son of a prominent Iranian-American family.

His friends came to me and said, "Could we have a memorial service at All Souls?" It turned out there was no place in the city where they felt they could have an adequate memorial service except here, and I said, "Absolutely, let's have it here." They asked, "Would I mind if it were three hours long?" I gulped a bit and tried to picture how I would fill three hours in a memorial service.

But they said, "There'll be other people to help on this. People will speak in Pharsee, we'll have nice music, people may sit quietly through the bulk of the service or they may get up and walk around, because in Iran at a memorial service everyone talks to each other all the time. We don't know whether all these adults who come are going to want to talk to each other and it's going to be noisy, or whether they're all going to sit here quietly."

I must tell you that when I came in at one point in the service there was not a seat available in this sanctuary, and it was so quiet that if I had closed my eyes I would have thought I was in an empty room. They weren't even rustling their clothes. That's how quiet it was.

They had speakers. They had nice music, and they spoke about the boy. At the end a string quartet played the distinctly Christian "Ave Maria." I was horrified. I wondered who had decided that the "Ave Maria" should be played. As gently as I could I asked the string quartet, "Why did you play the 'Ave Maria'?" They said, "Because the mother of the boy wanted that played at the end of the service."

That told me something I had long since forgotten—that Jesus is an important person in the history of Islam. He's highly regarded. In fact, the symbol of Mary, his mother, is very important in Islam. So I was reminded of something I should have known.

Finally, my wife and I were in Nepal, India, and Pakistan last fall. All three countries have many Muslims. However, Pakistan is the distinctly Muslim country; almost everyone there is Muslim.

We had two days in Pakistan. The first day was the day after Mrs. Butto lost her election, and feeling ran deep that day. On the second day we were there, all the provincial offices were being voted on. The campaign trucks and politicians with their megaphones were up and down the streets. We walked over a good stretch of Lahore. The politicians even let us go into a polling booth and watch the voting, which surprised me, since we were westerners.

But what interested me most about our experience in Pakistan was our guide, Rafiq. I have never in my life met as intense a person as Rafiq. From the moment he saw us he began talking to us about

Islam—the history of his country, just continuous, continuous, continuous. He began on the bus with a prayer that we all get back safely. Well, we could go along with that.

Then he went on and on about why they do what they do. One of our tour people referred to him very quietly as "Motormouth," because he never stopped talking. Some of our people had enough of him. But Polly and I said, "This is exactly what we came to Pakistan for, to hear what these people think." We felt we received a wonderful education in two days.

I wanted to take issue with him regarding some of the things he said. One was that there are seventy diseases that are controllable by diet alone. I wanted to ask him what the seventy are. I believe in good diet to some extent, but I can't imagine that all of the diseases I am afraid of could be controlled by diet. But that's what he thought.

Then I tried a kind of tricky question, one that was a little sensitive. I asked, "How many people in Pakistan have AIDS?" His answer, "Not a single one!" I had trouble believing that. We had seen people in the mosques with needles, for instance. The drug culture is big in parts of Pakistan. So I couldn't believe what he was saying. I didn't challenge him too much on it, because we were in his country, but I didn't agree with everything he said.

I also developed an appreciation for some of the things he did say. One was that all these rules, which one assumes are hard and fast rules in Islam, are really suggestions of what people should do. In fact, he said, you don't have to pray five times a day, or whatever. If you can't get to Mecca in your lifetime because you are poor, there are other ways—you go to another place close to home, for example.

He had a legalistic view of the rights and wrongs in life. I could understand a lot of what he was saying, and I took hope from the fact that he said that nothing is so ironclad that you can't break it if reason tells you that it has to be broken.

I liked the fact that he seemed to appreciate Akbar, one of the emperors of India, who was a great intellectual. Akbar, although he was Muslim, had three wives—one Christian, one Muslim, and the other Hindu. I guess Akbar wanted to have all the best influences in his life. He surrounded himself with intellectuals, people of many backgrounds; I dubbed Akbar, the "Unitarian Universalist without knowing it." He was ahead of his time, to my thinking.

He built temples, for instance, and whereas Muslims were not to have any animal representations in their sculpture, he had animals carved into the temples. Subsequently, another Mogul came along and cut all the heads off all the animals. Visitors see these temples in India with all the heads missing on animals. Peoples' ideas changed.

We learned something about Islam last summer.

I've also learned a great deal from Peter Awn from Columbia University, who was here teaching an adult education course and gave three lectures recently. He's dynamic, wonderful.

Peter made a point in his lectures that the variety of belief and practice within Islam is simply incredible. We shouldn't for a moment lump Muslims together. We can't do it, any more than we can lump Roman Catholics together and say that there isn't much difference between an Irish Catholic and a Filipino Catholic, or say there's not much difference in Protestantism between a German Lutheran and a Latin American Pentecostal.

There are enormous differences in Islam and in various countries. We continue to learn at All Souls, by visiting the mosque on 96th Street, by teaching in PS 151, where many of the children are from Muslim families, and by reading the newspapers with a new intentionality, to be better informed about a huge portion of the world's people.

I once knew many things about Islam that I had begun to forget. We can learn many more things than we have even guessed at.

I had begun to forget that "Allah" is simply the Arabic word for "God," and that when a Muslim prays to Allah, the person assumes that he or she is praying to the same god as are Christians and Jews. We Unitarian Universalists have been saying again and again that the word "God" is a human invention to describe something that is "above and beyond description." Can we doubt for a moment that the prayers of the Muslim are as important to God as are ours, we who do not happen to use the Arabic tongue? Or that we cannot worship as easily in a mosque as in a temple or church or by a lake?

Wouldn't it be ironic if Muslims thought all along they were praying to our god, but we didn't think we were praying to theirs?

I'm hoping that a number of us will make it a personal project to understand Islam better and also the Arabic world.

Tough issues must be wrestled with. If women's rights concern us, let us remember that women have a long way to go in western society as well. If the brutality of Saddam Hussein seems too much to even understand, let us remember that Hitler also practiced genocide, in the west. The upshot of our "clean" war against Iraq may be the awful deaths of millions of people who want to live as much as you and I do.

This is a great moment of opportunity. The new order that President George H. Bush talks about is going to be hammered out in foreign places, but also in *our* cities, where we rub shoulders and do business every day with representatives of all the world's religions and those of no religion.

What happens in a chess class, in a scout troop, or in an adult education class can build the bridges that the world desperately needs to avoid even worse catastrophes.

Let us realize that we are all bound by the same universe and struggling to understand it by whatever name, and that we must continually go out of our way to look into the mysteries around us.

My prayer today is that we can jointly make an effort to know better the people we know least.

Amen.

WHEN DEATH COMES HOME

READING

"I Think Continually Of Those"

I think continually of those who were truly great,

Who, from the womb,
remembered the soul's history
through corridors of light where
the hours are suns,
endless and singing,

Whose lovely ambition was that their lips,
still touched with fire,
should tell of the spirit clothed from head
to foot in song,

And who hoarded from the spring branches
the desires falling across their bodies like
blossoms.

What is precious is never to forget
the essential delight of the blood drawn
from ageless springs breaking through rocks
in worlds before our earth;

Never to deny its pleasure in
the simple morning light,
nor its grave evening demand for love;

Never to allow gradually the traffic to smother
with noise and fog the flowering of the spirit.

Near the snow, near the sun, in the highest fields
see how these names are feted by the waving

grass and by the streamers of white cloud and
whispers of wind in the listening sky:

The names of those who in their lives fought for
life, who wore at their hearts the fire's center.

Born of the sun they traveled a short while
towards the sun and left the vivid air signed
with their honor.

—Stephen Spender

SERMON
August 26, 1990

Christmas is normally a happy time of the year. Our family has a long history of celebrating that holiday with great joy and enthusiasm.

But the last two Christmases have been ones of considerable sadness for Polly and me, interrupted by death coming right to our door.

In 1988, four days before Christmas, Pan Am Flight 103 was blown up over Scotland, taking all 258 passengers to their death, including Kate Augusta Hollister. Kate had been our next-door neighbor from the day she was brought home as a baby from the hospital until her family had moved to Queens in 1987. In 1988 she was one of thirty-five college students aboard the flight coming home for Christmas.

Her parents asked me to conduct her memorial service at the United Nations Chapel. Many weeks later I also did the interment service at the cemetery. Her body was among the last to be recovered from the crash site. Then in June of 1989, I conducted a service at the placing of her gravestone.

Last year we approached Christmas knowing that my mother was incurably ill and might or might not make it to the holiday. She died in my sister's home in Rye, New York, on December 16. I conducted the memorial service on December 21, the year's anniversary of the Pan Am disaster.

Because I am a sixty-two-year-old clergyman, you might think I could take these two events in stride, having led hundreds of funeral and memorial services over thirty-eight years. The fact is, one is never fully prepared to experience the depth of emotion in someone who has lost a loved one, or when death knocks at your own door, as it is doing for so many these days.

You might be interested to know that only once in my ministry have I been called upon to tell someone (in this case two parents, back in the 1950s) that a family member (in that case their only child) had suddenly died. I remember it as if it were yesterday, going to their home, being greeted warmly by the unsuspecting parents, and having to break the news, as they say, about their daughter's heart attack.

The fact that in my long ministry I've been asked to do that only once raises questions for me. What does it say about the ministry? Or my ministry? In the moment of confronting Jane's unsuspecting parents, I developed a great respect for the policeman, who has to stand in that spot many times in his career.

But apart from that, I have seen death arrive many times, at the beds of the elderly and also in the most untimely places and situations.

Still, I felt almost completely unprepared for Kate Hollister's service, for coping with the loss of someone I knew well, the outpouring of feelings from her family and friends, where she was the victim not of accident or of natural causes, but of murder by international terrorists.

When I noticed in *The New York Times* that a service was going to be held at the United Nations Chapel for another victim of Pan Am 103 the day before Kate's services, I decided to attend it also, to see what kinds of things would be said, even to get an idea how the presiding clergyman might handle an impossibly large crowd, which was also likely to be the case for Kate's service.

I attended that service the day before. Hundreds were present, jamming every bit of space. I came away from that service as angry as I ever get, also reassured that whatever I did the next day for Kate would be vastly superior to what I had just witnessed.

The service was conducted by a clergyman of one of the Protestant denominations—it could have been Methodist or Episcopalian. Mercifully, I don't remember even the denomination, much less the clergyman's name.

He stood at the central lectern, bathed in light throughout, tossing out Christian platitudes and readings without mentioning the deceased by name, much less telling us anything about him or his family or even referring to the fact that he had died in a disaster.

The one fact about the deceased I was able to infer was that he must have gone to Yale, because an announcement was made at the end that a reception following the service would be held at the Yale Club! If the man had a wife or children present at the memorial service, some of us never found out.

I came away saying, "Tomorrow just do *exactly the opposite* of everything you just saw today!" And I did, to the best of my ability.

I conducted Kate's service seated, almost in the dark, way off to one side. Where the clergyman had stood the day before was a lovely photograph of Kate. The music consisted of the pieces she liked best, some on organ, some recordings, including Bruce Springsteen and Ravel's *Pavanne for a Dead Princess*, which I will never hear again without thinking of Kate.

I did give a eulogy, again from the dark, composed of bits and pieces of information that the family and her closest friend had given me in the days just previously. Included were the doorman's recollection of her trip home from the hospital as a baby twenty years earlier. I included the smacks on the head by her older brother, the asthma, her love of soap operas, Chinese food, shopping, the Museum of Natural History, and chocolates.

The readings included the Stephen Spender poem we read this morning. Needless to say, I found it difficult to conclude the Spender one, thinking about the explosion at 32,000 feet, thinking about the fire, the pain, possibly the conscious falling five miles to the earth.

The reading concludes, if you remember: "Near the snow, near the sun, in the highest fields, see how these names are feted by the waving grass and the streamers of white cloud and whispers of wind in the listening sky: the names of those who, in their lives, fought for life, who wore at their hearts the fire's center. Born of the sun, they traveled a short while towards the sun, and left the vivid air signed with their honor."

Last fall, when we realized that my mother wasn't going to make it, after eighty-four years of splendid health, Kate and her family had already helped me to cross one bridge, and that was figuring out what ideally should happen in a memorial service.

Still, the last several weeks were very difficult ones, with mother at my sister's place in Rye, and Polly and me many going back and forth after work.

Things almost never go the way one expects them to go. One has a kind of idealized notion of perhaps being at the bedside of a dying parent, holding hands, and having a final unburdening of hearts on both sides that brings a measure of peace and reconciliation. At the moment my mother died I was eating alone in a Chinese restaurant on Third Avenue, far from her bed in Rye, New York. I had no idea that she was breathing her last. I had my violin with me, heading to play in a concert that night.

By the time Polly and I met before the concert, Polly knew that mother was gone, but wisely let me play the concert before she told me.

Looking back, there were many ironies. Our soloist that night was pianist Norman Krieger, and his major piece in the concert was Gershwin's *Rhapsody in Blue*. That is the one piece my parents had to hear me play over and over and over on the piano in my teens because I was determined to master it. And when I learned after the concert that my mother had died just before the concert, I had this unavoidable image of her soul, now free and happy, finding its way to the concert and having to hear the *Rhapsody in Blue* one more time, while I played in the orchestra.

The next day my sister said, half jokingly, "I guess you're in charge of the service, since you're the only clergyman around!" I was not terribly surprised or dismayed.

Sixteen of us met at the chapel in Rye for mother's service, all family, since her friends were in Detroit.

I had put the sixteen chairs in a circle, but without them being obviously in a circle—some were in a little farther, some back a bit, but there was no leader's chair, or a chair where one could comfortably feel oneself to be only a spectator. It was a very studied, casual arrangement. We made liberal use of pictures on the tables and beside the casket. Everyone was surprised when my mother's brother and his wife from California walked in. And we found ourselves talking very soon about what made mother an absolutely unique person, as is indeed every person. The service was full of humor. Someone recalled how mother used to tell jokes and not be able to deliver the punch line. We remembered Louise and her laughing all the way to Italy on a darkened airplane while the passengers were trying to sleep, and Polly and I had shuddered in the "no smoking" section up ahead. Mother was a pretty happy person and that came through in the memorial service.

In fact, we simply adjourned after an hour, following a reading from the book of Proverbs, went to a restaurant and continued our lively discussion. We left feeling that the best part of my mother had been present at the service and would continue in all of our memories, and that was enough.

The loss of one's last surviving parent does move one up to the top of the ladder, as Forrest and many others have noted. Next week at our family reunion in Ocean City, New Jersey, twenty-five of us will be gathered for four days. For the first time Polly and I will be the seniors. who must be honored or flouted by two other generations, as they see fit.

I received a letter recently from a friend who had lost his wife. Both he and his wife were confirmed humanists.

In the period after her death he had talked to a Unitarian minister and had asked the question, "What consolation is there for a Unitarian at a time like this?" He continued, "I knew it was a rhetorical question. What consolation, indeed?"

He said, "I fully agree with the various authors writing on death and dying the nonreligious way. It isn't worse or easier for humanists, but in place of meaningless ritual and illusory promise of an afterlife, we *can* find purpose and solace."

He continued, "As the days passed, I realized that I needed something positive to replace the self-destructive grief and anger that had engulfed me after my wife's death. Because she had always been such a positive, upbeat person, I knew she would not have wanted me to mourn her as I was doing."

I empathize so much with that man. The last thing I want to provide, or have someone else provide, is meaningless ritual. And I see a promise of afterlife as illusory—none of us has been there and back. (On occasion a person on his or her deathbed has demanded to know if I believed in life after death. I have been content to say something like, "We only experience life. We don't need to fear what we won't experience.")

I guess the sentence that bothers me in my friend's letter is the one that refers to "dying the non-religious way."

Does that mean "without seeing an individual's death in any context or philosophy of what life *is*, and *about*?" Does it mean "no memorial service, just an obit in the newspaper?" Does it mean "discouraging people from getting together as a group to think about the deceased, about what things are important and what things are not important in the person who's gone and in oneself?"

How much better, it seems to me, to provide an opportunity for people to speak, and consequently, for something of the deceased to live on more than if it had not been shared.

I realize I chose a rather heavy topic this morning, "When Death Comes Home," partly because death *did* come home to Polly and me. I needed to share feelings with you, and partly because the world situation suggests we may all be called upon to deal with the subject in the days ahead.

I come out reinforced in the feeling that as long as we have others to share with, we will discover that all is not lost when someone dies, that an individual's life can continue to carry on, and that the best part of a person lives on in us.

Also, when we share fully with others, we find that our situation is really very close to everyone else's. The Donald Trumps of the world put their shoes on, first one and then the other, as we do, and the homeless know periods of great exultation, just as we do. The Iraqis have bodies just as miraculous as our own. I'm convinced that the number of people in the world who relish the idea of their involvement in war must be infinitesimally small.

We learn these things when we communicate with others. Countries, like individuals, must communicate more.

A church exists because people need to share the best and the worst with each other, they need to think about how the best and the worst have been dealt with in the past, by religious leaders and by common people. That's why we're here this morning. We can exult in Sandy Caron's successful liver transplant, and we can talk about peace in the Middle East, which we did in chapel last Wednesday evening.

We are a body of the "concerned." In the very difficult days ahead I plead that we recognize what a healing community we can be for one another if we are willing to open our hearts.

To life!

Amen.

"WHAT DIZZY DEAN TAUGHT ME"

READING

This reading is by Paul Carnes, a former president of the Unitarian Universalist Association, who died too young, while still in office. He wrote:

> I have always found myself backing off from the proposition that values were totally human inventions—that they represented choices, or preferences, without reference to anything that transcended humankind.
>
> A recent bout with the flu convinced me. We make our choices within and against—in response to—a larger reality. This reality both supports freedom and limits it.
>
> It came to me, not very originally to be sure, that we live on a stage. We are actors, but we are limited by the stage, and we must always be aware that our acting may be considerably altered if a board from the floor comes up suddenly and smacks us in the face.
>
> So what is the nature of that reality? It is...life producing and freedom producing. (It is also life limiting and freedom limiting.)
>
> Isn't it marvelous Job was able to say, "Though God slay me, yet I will love God."

SERMON
August 27, 1989

In 1934 I was seven years old and growing up in Detroit in a middle-class family.

My father's insurance office was on the top floor of a building not far from Navin Field, the baseball home of the Detroit Tigers. Navin Field would later become Briggs Stadium, and finally Tiger Stadium, each time with vast improvements. The Tigers today play on the same spot where I saw them play more than fifty years ago.

From Dad's office we couldn't quite see down onto the playing field six blocks away, but we could see and hear the crowd. When Charley Gehringer, Hank Greenberg, or one of the other Detroiters hit one out of the ballpark into Cherry Street or Michigan Avenue, you didn't have to have a radio on to know that a big rally was in progress. Needless to say, I enjoyed the occasional trip to my dad's office and hearing the roar of the crowd.

In 1934 I saw my first "real" baseball game. Television was still a long way off, and I had no idea what the inside of a ballpark looked like. One of the strongest memories I have as a child is walking up the ramp with my father, hand in hand, wondering what in the world a ballpark looked like, and seeing for the first time the infield, and the outfield, and the teams working out on them, and hearing the click of the bat against the ball. Above all, I saw a shade of green that I didn't know existed. I've never seen the top of a billiard table that looked greener than Navin Field in the sunshine that day.

But 1934 was a special year for the Tigers. They made it into the World Series for the first time in almost thirty years—since the days of Ty Cobb. By September no other subject was worth discussing in town than the fortunes of the Tigers.

That same September I entered second grade in Bagley Elementary School. The boys were caught up in pennant fever, and the girls, if they were smart, were learning the rules of the game as fast as they could.

The Tigers drew as their opponents in the World Series the St. Louis Cardinals. I can even say the "hated" St. Louis Cardinals, because it was generally agreed, at least in Detroit, that the Cardinals were the meanest, most uncivilized group of athletes ever brought together on one team, deserving and relishing their nickname, "The Gashouse Gang." Their players had names like "Ducky" Medwick, Frankie Frisch, "Pepper" Martin, Leo "The Lip" Durocher. And they had the greatest pitching combination of two brothers in the history of baseball in Paul and Dizzy Dean, who between them had already won fifty games that year.

For game one of the World Series, every classroom in Bagley School had a radio, probably excepting the kindergarten. At game time all instruction ceased, and we sat at our desks groaning or cheering with every pitch.

The Tigers won the first game. Clearly the better team was asserting itself! All radios were in place the next day, and the Tigers lost, much to our dismay. But the third game went to the Tigers, and we were a step closer to the championship. St. Louis won the fourth game, but the Tigers won the fifth. Now we needed just one more win and virtue would be triumphant.

When Detroit lost the sixth game, it hardly seemed to matter. In fact, it seemed quite in the pattern of things. The next day we had our best pitcher going against Dizzy Dean, whom we had already defeated once, if memory serves me.

Let me digress a moment.

It is just to say that the principal activity of a seven-year-old, it seems to me, is figuring out how things work. It may be true for all children and adults at any age, but I know it is true for seven-year-olds.

Everybody in the second grade had sort of figured something out simultaneously—that the Tigers were at least capable of winning every other day, and that the Cardinals were incapable of winning two games in a row and thus doing more than temporarily drawing even every other day. The stage was set for the final victory, for the triumph of good over evil, our guys against their guys. (I'm sure we were learning in Sunday school at that time that "good triumphs over evil.") We were part of a huge cosmic plot, where the Ducky Medwicks of the world would be put in their place.

Need I say? On the afternoon of the seventh and final game, the second graders at Bagley School listened, first in disbelief, then in abject horror, as the Cardinals pushed across run after run after run after run!

The final score was St. Louis: 11; Detroit: nothing!

And I mean: nothing! Evil had triumphed over good, and triumphed big! Dizzy Dean had humbled us all.

To a person we sat at our desks and cried. The teacher cried to see us crying, and we cried to see the teacher crying. What a disconsolate bunch of children stumbled home from school that day to meet their grieving parents!

In retrospect, one can laugh a lot about the disproportionate amount of emotion we second graders expended on a baseball World Series, compared to what proved to be the larger issues of the day—the Depression, the rise of Hitler, the gathering war clouds.

I don't think it occurred, even for a moment, to any of us that the children in elementary schools in Missouri might be going out of their minds with elation—their Cardinals had broken the pattern on the seventh day, and confirmed the victory of good over evil by smacking down the terrible Tigers!

But I do know that Dizzy Dean taught me a lesson that has come back to me again and again over the years, since the trauma of the 1934 Series has partially abated.

The lesson is this: We think we understand. We see patterns in events. We assume causal connection because we see the pattern. But particularly where human beings are concerned, (and even in the physical sciences, as the nineteenth century philosophers showed us), we may be in for a big surprise just when we think we understand something. As adults we have the same problem as second graders, perhaps more so, since our minds tend to become rigid.

Bob Kaufman, the minister who has just left the Universalist Church across the park, did an interesting experiment on the UU ministers at the General Assembly in New Haven in June. He asked us questions to which we were to respond quickly. Invariably he led us all to give wrong answers.

For example, he said, "Everyone count from 10 to 1 backwards!" We all said "10,9,8,7," etc. Of course, 10 to 1 backwards is "1,2,3,4," etc. (Think about it a bit.)

He asked, "Who was the greatest prize fighter who ever lived?" We shouted, "Joe Louis!" He asked, "What's the biggest city in Missouri?" We shouted, "St. Louis!" He asked, "What's the capital of Kentucky?" We all shouted, "Louisville!" (It's Frankfort.)

He asked, "What do you call a funny story?" We said, "A joke." He asked, "What do you call a jab in the ribs?" We said, "A poke." He asked, "What do you call the white of an egg?" We shouted, "A yoke!" And then realized that the yoke is the yellow part of an egg. He had a whole string of those mind twisters, and even though we knew what he was doing to us, we couldn't break our patterns of response.

His point was to show that a person cannot give "knee-jerk" reactions to situations and still be a thinking entity. Similarly, the complex questions that surround us on abortion, animal rights, disarmament, the environment, and relations with other countries all defy simple answers. (I loved it when he said, "At least in any liberal group you can't get two knees to jerk at the same time in the same direction.") I thought the ministers came pretty close to it in his experiments with us.

But life is complicated. We have to take stands based on our understandings and the thought processes we have built up, and at the same time recognize that we have a limited point of view and someday may see things in an entirely different light.

When Polly and I were in Alaska in 1983, we were on a bus tour of Ketchikan. You have to realize that while Ketchikan has many miles of roads to outlying places, none of the roads connect with the outside world because of the rugged terrain. Consequently, just about all the food supplies for this good-sized city arrive once a week on a barge from Seattle.

Our bus driver was a woman about twenty-five years old. She told us that when she was a child the family lived twenty miles away. A few times a year they would all get dressed up and drive in to Ketchikan. "I thought Ketchikan was the center of the world," she said. She added, "It's only when I started driving this bus and talking to tourists that I realized that Ketchikan is nowhere!"

Part of growing up is learning what a limited point of view we have.

It's not only that Ketchikan, Detroit, or even New York is not the center of the universe geographically. It's that, for instance, Unitarian Universalists make up one tenth of one percent of the population in this country; or that the United States would just about fit into the Sahara Desert or Australia, or several times into Russian Siberia. It's also learning that we are the biggest debtor nation in the world, the greatest polluter, and the greatest consumer of natural resources.

"Growing up" is learning that values we have always accepted as normal and desirable for humankind may be held by a declining minority even in our own country or community.

While I was a minister at the Community Church of New York I once found myself quite by accident in the middle of a case where a policeman was charged with molesting two early-teenage girls. My involvement came from the fact that I happened to be waiting for an elevator when the policeman in question walked out of their apartment around midnight, and I could attest beyond any shadow of a doubt in my mind that a uniformed policeman had been in their apartment.

I remember that a woman member of Community Church, intelligent and informed in many ways, could not accept in her mind the possibility that a policeman could be guilty of such an act. Here was her own minister, telling her something that shook her faith in people and society. That was in the mid-1960s. Today most of us are sophisticated enough to know that the so-called pillars of society are unfortunately sometimes also the scalawags.

I often think about that woman, how her view of how the community and world functions was shattered, and hopefully enlarged ultimately, by what I had to tell her. We continually come to these watersheds where the patterns we have counted on, the systems we have built up in our minds to explain things and give us security, simply can no longer do the job in the face of reality.

Each of these watersheds affects our religious outlook on life. A child's image of the world is apt to include a God not unlike one or both of his or her parents, as an explanation of "what makes things happen." In normal growth the child has to revise both the importance of parents in "what makes things happen," and also the role of a deity, who tends to become more and more remote and less capable of being manipulated.

We go through the most painful, but also liberating, experiences, as we learn that no person, or group, or religious body (not even Unitarians) can give us half-complete answers to the practical problems that beset us.

But we cannot "go it alone" either, in life, because that is to take the most provincial position of all, and to limit extremely our possibilities for future growth.

So we join with others who are also willing to do some learning as they go along, who know pretty well what they believe, but can allow that most of the world sees things quite differently, and that they too will change in time, hopefully with a broader, more inclusive view that permits them to be of greater service to humanity as a whole, and to their dearest ones.

The world is chock full of surprises, at least for Polly and me. Presidents Nixon and Reagan were not my choices at the ballot box, but Nixon pleasantly surprised me with his overtures to China and Reagan with his reaching out to Russia.

Some of the surprises have been appalling, like the advent of AIDS, and modern medicine's inability so far to find good answers to AIDS, or the arrival of the homeless on our streets, linking us with third world countries in that regard, or the discovery that each stealth bomber will cost us 600 million dollars!

However, some of the surprises are rewarding beyond our wildest expectations.

I can't help mentioning our country's success this past week in photographing the planet Neptune and its moon, Triton, from a satellite launched twelve years ago, whose original purpose was to take it, in four years, from Jupiter to Saturn. By now I'm sure we are all aware that while it was in flight, the plan was concocted to send it also to Uranus and Neptune, more than a billion miles and eight years later.

This week it sent back to us all those pictures on twenty-two watts of energy, the amount that would light your refrigerator bulb. The signal strength reaching the earth was a fraction of a billionth of a watt. Add to that the problem of the light level on Neptune being a hundred times dimmer than on earth, memory loss from aging computers, gears that don't work well anymore, and a host of other complications, and one can only stand in awe of science's achievement. As I say, many of our surprises in life are rewarding beyond anything we could have imagined.

In spite of my sermon title this morning being, "What Dizzy Dean Taught Me," I don't regard this as a sermon about baseball.

My thought was to let a story from the world of baseball symbolize how a seven-year-old may suffer a loss of innocence about his own capability to figure things out. The world is far more complex at any point in our life than we can appreciate. Part of wisdom is realizing that we can be most wrong when we feel most certain about something.

We come up against that hard "reality" of which Paul Carnes wrote, the reality that gives us our freedom and also limits it. Sometimes the board on the stage comes up and hits us in the face. Sometimes even our most faltering efforts are acclaimed a huge success.

A part of wisdom is seeing the huge potential in every human being, including ourselves, while also realizing how imperfect our vision may be, as well as everyone else's.

In the year 1638, more than 350 years ago, the Swedes launched the largest warship ever built, the Vasa. The crowds surrounded the main harbor in Stockholm. While the bands played and its 437 crewmen stood at attention, the ship slid down the ways, floated out into the harbor, caught the first breeze, turned upside down, and sank.

Now that *WAS* a surprise!

Prayer: As this new season comes upon us, we seek strength for ourselves and for this congregation, and for the world community. Knowing that change is continually with us, may the spirit of love, and appreciation, and humility, continue to hold us and our world together. Amen.

Footnote, in the year 2004: After this sermon was delivered in 1989, the Rev. Darrell Berger of the Fourth Universalist Church of New York, himself a dedicated student of baseball, pointed out a basic inaccuracy in this sermon. The seven games mentioned were not won alternatively by the two teams through game six, contrary to the memory I had nursed since childhood.

But because the sermon was my "most remembered sermon" apparently by members of the All Souls congregation, it was reprinted here in its original form, including the incorrect order of wins and losses.

Thank you, Darrell, for illustrating the very point of this sermon, that a memory cherished for more than fifty years can crunch hard against the even harder rock of "reality!"

RDL

The Great Strainer of Naturalness

READING

A New York Times Review, June 18, 1987

Elliot Finkel, who made his New York debut Monday evening in Weil Recital Hall, was an endearing presence onstage when he wasn't roughing up the piano. A graduate of the Mannes and Juilliard Schools of Music and a student of Josef Raleff, Mr. Finkel performed works by Schubert, Glazunov and Scriabin and a set of jazz-related pieces by Gershwin, Oscar Levant and Billy Mayerl. The latter group inspired the artist's most sympathetic playing, particularly the four short works by Mayerl, which Mr. Finkel rendered gently, breezily, and with spirited abandon.

Often the pianist's high spirits got the better of him. Mr. Finkel is a large man, and when he set his mind to playing loudly, which he did at the slightest opportunity, it was a fearsome display. His interpretations sounded rough, not in terms of dropped notes but in the absence of tonal refinement, subtlety of phrasing and dynamic gradation. Mr. Finkel seemed to view the works in black and white terms—all soft passages were soft in the same way, and fast passages were zipped through as swiftly as possible, as if the performer couldn't wait to show his listeners just how quickly his fingers could move.

To his credit, he relished the act of playing the piano, got genuinely wrapped up in the music and conveyed his enthusiasm to his listeners. Mr. Finkel ended pieces by turning to the crowd even before the sound of the last note had died away, and smiling, as if to ask, "Wasn't that nice?"

From him it seemed somehow unaffected, and his supportive audience answered with warm applause.

—Review by Michael Kimmelman

SERMON
July 5, 1987

Almost twenty years ago, when Polly was breaking into the banking world as a teller at Citibank, at their Park Avenue and 57th Street branch, she was amazed one day when a rather small man presented himself at her window and gave her a check signed "Arthur Rubinstein." Recognizing the great pianist, she said, "Mr. Rubinstein, it is a great pleasure meeting you; my husband and I have been admirers of yours for many years."

To which he beamed and reached his right hand through the bars of the teller's cage to shake Polly's hand.

She was flabbergasted by his gesture of friendship—he had actually placed in her hand one of the hands that performed for millions and millions of people in every country of the world!

I have to say that Polly acted the way any normal teenager would have done (though she was forty at the time), holding her hand aloof the rest of the day, not wanting to touch any other hand with the hand that had shaken Arthur Rubinstein's.

"It's funny," she told me later, "he had a firm grip for a man of about seventy, but it didn't seem to be a large hand. It made you wonder how he plays such incredible passages with such strength."

When the movie of his life came out, appropriately entitled *Love of Life*, we saw it three times. When his autobiography was published, we read it from cover to cover. Things that he said crept into my sermons.

He became for me almost a mystical figure, the great artist, a person so completely in tune with life and so in love with life that he could give completely of himself to others, and at the same time take into himself all that life had to offer.

When he died a few years later, it was like losing a member of the family.

Only recently, however, I came across this quotation about Arthur Rubinstein by the pianist Daniel Barenboem, which sort of says it all. He says of Rubinstein, "His playing had a great naturalness. Any ideas he had about playing a piece he put through a great strainer of naturalness in his mind. Nothing seemed forced or willed."

It is that "great strainer of naturalness" that I would like us to think about this morning.

Many of my lessons in life come from the world of music. I've had the privilege of singing under the great choral conductor Robert Shaw, as have some of you. I was fascinated once to hear him say that when he gets an unfamiliar musical score, he simply goes over and over that score in his head, trying every conceivable tempo and nuance.

He whistles it on subways, sings it on a park bench, trying different shadings and dynamics, and slowly there emerges for him the only possible way the piece could be played or sung. In other words, he has run the piece through a great strainer of naturalness for him, and come up with the only interpretation that makes sense to him.

I see the same greatness in the cellist Yo Yo Ma, who played recently at a wedding I performed at the United Nations. Before the wedding, he practiced a bit while standing up, and the music was as fine as I've heard from any cellist sitting down! Then he asked if I had seen his accompanist. I said, "I think he went downstairs to the men's room," and I took several steps in that direction to hurry him back. To my complete amazement Mr. Ma raced past me and went bounding down the flight of stairs, two at a time, with his precious instrument held in one hand! The man has so much energy that it comes pouring out in every conceivable direction, and incomparably through his cello. Does he know something we don't know?

I even see it in Elliot Finkel, who was the subject of one of the readings this morning, and his brother Ian, the professional xylophone player, who claims he can play all of the standard violin concertos on the xylophone. Polly and I have heard him play, and we have no reason to doubt him. He looks a bit like a madman, but he plays the instrument as it has never been played before.

The examples are all around us, in all walks of life. Is there anybody who doesn't respond affirmatively to what the Flying Karamazov Brothers do? I don't care whether you prefer them in their own act or as part of a Shakespearean comedy. If you can't thrill to their incredible skills and their self-enjoyment as they "do their thing," you should look hard for the reason why.

Jesus once said, "Except as you become little children, you shall in no way enter the kingdom of heaven." That verse has been interpreted and reinterpreted as much as any verse in the Bible. However you cut it, it says that children have something on the rest of us that we probably lost along the way and they are in danger of losing.

That something, for me, is the sense of the complete open-endedness of life, that the future can be anything, that the possibilities in each of us, and those close to and far from us, are beyond imagining. Children assume it, and they are right. We've forgotten that we can play all the possible themes in life in all possible ways, and come up with what is natural for us.

Henry David Thoreau said in the last century:

> I wish to live deliberately, to front only the essential
> facts of life.
> I wish to learn what life has to teach, and not, when I come
> to die, discover that I have not lived.
> I do not wish to live what is not life, living is so dear.
> Nor do I wish to practice resignation, unless it is
> quite necessary.
> I wish to live deep and suck out all the marrow of life, to
> live so sturdily as to put to rout all that is not life;
> I want to cut a broad swath, and shave close, to drive life
> into a corner, and reduce it to its lowest terms.
> If it proves to be mean, then to get the whole and genuine
> meanness of it, and publish its meanness to the world;

> Or if it is sublime, to know it by experience, and be able to give a true account of it.

I imagine children everywhere can relate to those words, as can the child in us.

The hardest thing for me in the first twenty-five years of my life was to give up the violin as my likely profession.

I came to the Eastman School of Music at age sixteen as a real "hot-shot" violinist—in my own eyes. I had been the assistant concertmaster of the National High School Orchestra, and had medals to show for what seemed like endless hours of practice. My teacher at Eastman heard me play and announced that if I were going to play the violin seriously, I would have to unlearn the instrument and start all over again.

I knew he was right. He showed me how to hold the instrument; I didn't begin to hold it correctly to get the maximum freedom to move on it. To unlearn what, with poor teaching, had grooved thousands of times over in my head seemed an unbearable prospect.

And there was more. World War II was coming to an end, and none of the musicians seemed aware that we were in a war, or that the postwar world would be a challenge to every one of us.

I think I looked at a wall in my room for about two days, and more and more realized that I didn't even like the violin, that I had never liked it, but rather used it as a tool to impress people.

I didn't like opening the case, which always tended to stick closed. I didn't like putting on the shoulder pad, which could and did fall off from time to time, or worrying about the bow that accumulated grease from my hand where the knuckle touched it, as a reminder that I too often played the instrument with dirty hands, maybe immediately after a touch football game.

Or, God forbid, a string should have broken! Are you aware of the contortions a violinist must go though to replace an A string, where the holes in the key that needs to be threaded are buried inaccessibly up under the scroll of the instrument where no teen-age boy's hands can work effectively?

I thought of the recital I had played in at about age twelve, when I hooked the end of my bow into the lace skirt of my accompanist before I even got started. I lifted her skirt up in trying to get untangled, and then looked out over a sea of amused but unforgiving faces.

I decided, there in my room at Eastman, that the violin and I were never meant for each other, that every time I had picked up a violin, in my deepest self I had felt it to be an unnatural act, at least for one teenage male.

Well, that's how one becomes a clergyman! Now you know!

Incidentally, years later I went back to the violin and found it rather enjoyable, at least at the new level I was doing it. I play in an orchestra today that accompanies members of the Philharmonic; I enjoy being in charge of the second violin section of the orchestra.

Does it seem natural to play the violin? Well, I still have trouble with shoulder pads falling off, and grease collecting on my bow. But I kind of get a kick out of changing A strings that break. And every now and then in a concert I hear myself playing a tricky passage, and I hear it as from a distance, as if I were only a listener and not the player, and I have even said to myself with considerable admiration: "Hey! listen to that guy go!"

That has happened to me only in recent years.

The great strainer of naturalness. What is natural? What isn't natural? To be theological, what fits the laws of nature? What doesn't fit the laws of nature? Is "nature" much more open-ended than we've assumed? What are our individual natures? How can we bring ourselves more in tune with nature? With our natures?

Fred Astaire was once asked how he managed to do everything that he did. His answer was, "I just dance." Wouldn't it be nice if each one of us could say, "I just live."

What would it mean to the world if countries went about "just living"? Is it natural to build stockpiles of weapons for overkilling our neighbors?

If we look at the Declaration of Independence for a moment, we notice that for Jefferson and our forefathers there was an assumption about the natural order of things.

In Jefferson's day the phrase most often heard was "the right to life, liberty, and property." Jefferson substituted for the word *property* the phrase "the pursuit of happiness."

Social theorists later on tried to make much of Jefferson's dropping of the word *property*, as though he had an anticapitalist point of view. But such was not the case; Jefferson believed in private property as much as he believed in slavery as being in the natural order of things. The full egalitarianism of all human beings was an idea that was only beginning to form in the consciousness of humanity in 1776.

But it is still of great interest that Jefferson substituted "the pursuit of happiness" in place of "property." The substitution has been called "a characteristic and illuminating stroke on the part of this social philosopher, who throughout his life placed human rights first. If government fails to perform these functions, 'it is the right of the people to alter or abolish it altogether, and to institute new government'—as Americans were doing."

In listing the colonies' grievances against Great Britain (which in the Declaration are directed against the king, George the Third, although Parliament was more the culprit), the list begins with offenses against common sense, or we could say against the natural order of things:

> He (the king) has refused his assent to laws the most wholesome and necessary for the public good.
> He has forbidden his governors to pass laws of immediate and pressing importance, unless suspended in their operation till his assent should be obtained; and, when so suspended, he has utterly neglected to attend to them.
> He has called together legislative bodies at places unusual, uncomfortable, and distant from the depository of their public records, for the sole purpose of fatiguing them into compliance with his measures. (What kind of king

would do such unnatural things as making representatives meet at great distances from their records?)

The litany of abuses grows and becomes more strident.

He has erected a multitude of new offices, and sent hither swarms of new officers to harass our people and eat out their substance.

He has plundered our seas, ravaged our coasts, burnt our towns, and destroyed the lives of our people.

At this point Jefferson put in his sharpest criticisms of the king and Parliament, which were almost vitriolic, and most of which were omitted in the final version of the Declaration approved by the Continental Congress, phrases alluding to the king's "fostering treasonable insurrections of our fellow citizens," conducting himself like an infidel, committing murder, and Parliament permitting the Chief Magistrate to send over "not only soldiers of our common blood, but Scotch and foreign mercenaries to invade and destroy us. These facts have given the last stab to agonizing affection, and manly spirit bids us renounce forever these unfeeling brethren."

As I say, these sentiments didn't make it into the final Declaration. I can just hear Ben Franklin saying, "Tom, Tom, what you say is true, but there's no point in seeming to possibly overstate the case."

It is illuminating to look back at the Declaration of Independence as an interpretation of the natural order of things. It says basically: When things get too out of line with the natural order, people have to take steps to correct it.

It reflects a feeling that there is a natural orderliness to life, and also that the future is open-ended—we can take control of it, or at least appreciate it, together. We are bound together.

Religion tries to explain and explore this matter of belonging to a natural order with infinite possibilities. It often comes down heavy-footed, losing the joy, even the soul of what it means to be alive.

We begin to "fly" when we take ourselves more lightly, to use Forrest's wonderful observation.

Let me close with one more quotation, from Arthur Rubinstein, talking to Robert MacNeill on the MacNeill-Lehrer Hour. He says:

> What happens to me is something quite strange, which I observe very often. I observe the fact that I come on the stage for a concert...as a representation...I mean, as a picture of what happens on the stage, it is rather ridiculous, because a fat little man like me appearing there in an evening dress looks like an undertaker, you know, funeral—funeral things. And the piano has a little look of a coffin if you want to know.
>
> And...and the public...the public fills the hall, let's say. They come after a big dinner. The women look at each other or...at other women's dresses. Men think mostly about business or some games or some sports or God knows what. And there I have this crowd not entirely quite musical, not really knowers of music, but who like music, who love music.
>
> And that is a very difficult proposition. I have to hold them, you know, in attention, by my emotion—nothing else. I can't look at them, I can't make faces, I can't tell them...now comes a great moment, now you listen, now is a great thing for you...nothing of the kind. I have to play. Look there, straight in front of me. But there is a certain antenna...this is a certain secret thing. There is a thing which goes out, emanates from me, from my emotion...not from me...from my emotion, from the feeling, you like to call it "soul," if you like to.
>
> I don't know what soul means, but it is a word which one uses very much without knowing what it represents really. But this something which, let me call it for the moment "soul" if you like, projects something. Projects something which I do feel, I do feel that it is doing it. It suddenly puts the audience in my hands. There is a moment where I feel them all here. I can do anything. I can hold them as one little note in the air...they will not

breathe because they wait what happens next, you know, what will happen in the music. That is a great, great moment. Not always does it happen, but when it does happen, it is a great moment of our lives.

And I ask, "What more can we ask for than that we be in touch with our natural selves and the natural world around us?"

Frozen Bow Ties

READING

"Your children are the sons and daughters of life's longing
   for itself.
They come through you but not from you,
And though they are with you, yet they belong not to you.
You may give them your love, but not your thoughts,
For they have their own thoughts.
You may house their bodies but not their souls,
For their souls dwell in the house of tomorrow, which you
   cannot visit, not even in your dreams.
You may strive to be like them, but seek not to make them
   like you.
For life goes not backward nor tarries with yesterday.
You are the bows from which your children as living arrows
   are sent forth.

—Kahlil Gibran

SERMON
March 22, 1981

I'm aware that in picking a title for this morning's sermon I deliberately settled on one that would be intriguing—and unfathomable. I cannot in good conscience keep you in suspense any longer.

In one of three schools where I served as development officer after I left the Community Church in 1968, they had a sort of general store where textbooks were sold, as well as candy bars, ice cream, stickers and the like. The store was presided over by a middle-aged gentleman, whom I will call Mr. Jones, for the sake of anonymity. He was hard-working and very proper, and set himself apart a bit apparently by wearing a bow tie every day of his life.

One day one of the boys plunked down his money and asked for an ice cream sandwich. Mr. Jones reached deep into the ice cream bin and came up with the ice cream sandwich, but in so doing somehow dislodged his bow tie, which fell into the freezer.

Trying to recover his dignity and reattach the tie, he took an order from the next boy in line, who looked him squarely in the eye and without a trace of a smile, said, "I'll have a frozen bow tie."

Poor Mr. Jones. At that moment something must have snapped. He vaulted over the counter. The kid took off running down a long hall with Mr. Jones in hot pursuit. Whether or not he caught the boy is not recorded in anyone's memory. But what is known is that from that day on, if you were a boy in that school and wanted to demonstrate that you had limitless courage and were also a pretty good runner, you would walk up to Mr. Jones's counter in full view of your classmates, put your money down, look Mr. Jones in the eye, and say, "I'll have a frozen bow tie."

As a matter of fact, Mr. Jones finished out only that semester at the school and then, I suppose, moved on to another bookstore where he could try to forget the humiliation heaped on him by the students at our unnamed school.

That particular incident has always held a fascination for me, because it seems like a caricature of the problem that often exists between generations. For Mr. Jones, looking back at his humiliation, it must be easy to generalize that all the boys in the school were unmannered savages. And the boys, if any of them remember him several decades later, must think of him as particularly ill-humored and prissy.

Of course, the truth lies somewhere in between. And the irony of the situation is that such a simple event as dropping one's bow tie into a freezer could precipitate his giving up his job. If instead of being flustered he had been able to come up laughing, and taken the second boy's order as one of the funniest things a kid had ever thought of on the spur of the moment, how different his personal history might have been.

If you raise children of your own, or if you teach, you have to be ready for the frozen bow ties. If there is one thing that children are, they are individuals, with thoughts and purposes of their own, which as Gibran has said so well, "you cannot visit, even in your dreams."

One day a few years back I was on an 86th Street crosstown bus that had just pulled into the Central Park West bus stop before taking off across the park. It was a steamy summer's day. The bus was crowded and all the windows were open.

Standing on the bus near me was a derelict type, a white man, dirty and unshaven and rather full of alcohol.

I became aware that he was shaking his fist and half muttering at two little black boys on the sidewalk. They were neatly dressed, about ten years old, and each of them had just bought a Sabrett hot dog, loaded with mustard and sauerkraut. One of the boys in particular was gesturing as though he might throw the hot dog through the open window at the man snarling at them.

The man made one more gesture, accompanied by an oath. The kid took one more look at his expensive and appetizing hot dog, and then let it fly. Truer than a Nolan Ryan fastball it came, hitting the man right in the chest and spraying mustard and sauerkraut in all directions. (I can still see the sauerkraut hanging from the bus's ceiling.)

The man, only a couple of steps from the rear door, lunged at the door to give chase. The kids had already turned tail and were in full flight. But at that moment the driver, who may or may not have witnessed the whole affair, locked the rear door, took off through the park, and deposited the man on 5th Avenue and 84th Street.

Again, I was struck by how differently people could have interpreted that incident, depending on where they were, or what they had seen, or their predisposition to interpret an act of semi-violence, if we may call it that.

Some would have interpreted it, no doubt, as a racial incident. Maybe it was, to an extent, for the derelict and the boys. But I thought I saw a lot more there, including elements of class conflict.

The black children in this case interestingly representing the "haves" and the white derelict the "have not."

And there was the intergenerational aspect as well. As I look back on it, I am continually struck by the ability of a ten-year-old to forfeit a hot dog he had just paid good money for, in favor of what he perceived as rudimentary social justice.

Children simply refuse to be fitted into molds. My own children have picked professions and life styles that amaze me today. And I think back to the fact that my dad wanted me, more than anything, to go into the insurance business with him. It took him many years to get used to the fact that I was a clergyman. Some teachers in my elementary school apparently would have bet their fortune on the likelihood of my being strangled before I reached the age of eighteen.

However, apart from the fact that children are a continual source of surprise, of creativity, and of newness, the story of the frozen bow tie (and to a lesser extent the story of the missile hot dog) have taken on additional meaning for me over the years.

Mr. Jones has come to symbolize for me the adult who just became too rigid in his ways and was unable to adapt to a changing situation. Quite apart from his bow tie dropping into the freezer, there came a time when he no longer fit into his environment of running a store surrounded by high schoolers.

The bow tie itself could be seen as a symbol of maladaptation in a school where some of the faculty wore jeans. Mr. Jones reminded me of the impeccably dressed British in India sitting down to tea at 4 p.m., trying to preserve the customs of the homeland. (I'm not knocking bow ties as such, by the way—I wear them on occasion as seemingly called for and we all have idiosyncrasies, fortunately.)

I'm more worried about compulsive behavior that gives us more problems than we know how to handle.

We all live by customs, to an extent, which we have built up over many years, and which may be losing some of their relevance to the always changing present.

I have had the experience of watching senility claim many members of my own family. As a child I was surrounded by people who lived to a very old age, great-grandparents, great-aunts, and great-uncles. My dad's parents observed their fifty-seventh wedding anniversary, and my own parents their fifty-third. But that was nothing compared to Aunt Minnie and Uncle Ted, who had their sixty-seventh. My grandmother lived to ninety-three and was very sharp mentally. Uncle Ted lived to ninety-seven, but he didn't recognize anyone anymore. Still, he loved to perform a very comic routine involving his hat. The routine probably hadn't changed in eighty years, and he went nowhere, indoors or out, hot weather or cold, without wearing his hat and performing his hat act when the spirit moved him.

My father was only seventy-nine when he died, and for almost five years he didn't know who I was when I walked in the door.

When you are around that much senility, you become very sensitized, even as a child, to the symptoms, in others and in yourself. You remember hearing the same story told a hundred times by some member of the family. You remember which members of the family were more than satisfied with the way things were, who, more than anything, didn't want to see the *status quo* changed, as opposed to the family members who were eager to bring new things into their lives.

There were those who measured everything that happened in terms of how it affected them personally. And there were those who seemed to have a much wider window on the world, who were members of organizations, who espoused causes, who seemed able to help shape, and to be shaped by, the larger family of humankind. One learned at a tender age that while hardening of the arteries might play a part in senility, there was a psychological component as well.

I remember playing billiards with an aunt who was pretty good at the game. All of a sudden it dawned on me that when I was making my shots she was oblivious to me and was only thinking of her next one. I could make a difficult shot, albeit with some luck, and she would step up to the table for her next shot, completely unaware that I had made mine and was entitled to another. But if she made her shot, she expected me to join in her applause. And if she missed even by two feet, she expected me to groan with her.

That's probably why I didn't become a professional billiard player.

Like everyone else, I learned a great deal as a child from my family, and I am grateful to them for the values that became more evident as I grew older. Some of the lessons were also hard ones and not the ones they had intended. I live in almost morbid fear of telling the same story twice to the same person, so often did I hear the same stories through my youth.

Statistically, not many of us will become senile. And to encourage me, I have a fifty percent input from my mother's side of the family, where old age also prevailed, with little or no loss of mental ability.

Who among us can smugly say that we don't see the process of mental and emotional aging beginning in ourselves? In fact, one way to know that it is happening is not to be able to see it happening. If we are sensitive to the process, I believe we can take intelligent steps to counter it.

We can welcome new experience.

We can try harder to see things from another point of view.

We can suspend judgment on things we are not sure about.

One of my readings this morning was by Sophia Lyon Fahs, often described as the best theologian the Unitarians ever produced. To me the remarkable thing about Mrs. Fahs was not that she lived to the age of a hundred and two, which is remarkable enough, but that she didn't start writing until she was about sixty-five, and then she wrote not one, but a dozen first-rate books in the field of religious education. She also collaborated on others.

Old age need not be a time of withdrawal and self-pity; it can be the most exciting and rewarding time of life. She wrote, "Some beliefs are like walled gardens, they encourage exclusiveness and the feeling of being especially privileged." She could have said, "They are like frozen bow ties."

> Other beliefs are expansive and lead the way into wider and deeper sympathies.
> Other beliefs are rigid, like the body of death, impotent in a changing world,
> Other beliefs are pliable, like the young sapling, ever growing with the upward thrust of life.

She was talking about the beliefs of individuals and also the beliefs of institutions, because we do not operate in a vacuum. Our views are continually shaped by the institutions we are a part of—religious, political, academic. Institutions can suffer all the symptoms of aging and senility that we see in individuals.

I guess the thing I fear most in this world is that our country, indeed the major countries of the world, are suffering from institutional hardening of the arteries, that they are running on routines that served us once better than they serve us now.

I see the oldest U. S. president in history, and I hear themes played over and over again that seem to have little relevance to the world as it is in 1987, combined with a failure to cope seriously with emerging problems that could overwhelm all of humanity if they are not dealt with in time.

I worry about the rigid mind-sets of the Colonel Norths of this world, who substitute patriotism for understanding, who do not see that zealotry for any cause, including that of their country, puts them in the same class as those who forfeit their lives to bring down a Marine barracks in Lebanon, killing hundreds of human beings.

The problem is not ours alone. The Communist world has always been doctrinaire, and therefore rigid, and therefore in difficulty when confronted by change.

We have two friends, Jim and Gloria Stern, who have just come back from Russia, after having visited China on the way.

Their description of their experiences in the USSR match almost verbatim our experiences in Leningrad fourteen years ago—the number of soldiers and policemen on the street; the bureaucracy that permeates everything, from which taxicab you will be assigned to the exact spot where the cab will be met; the general sullenness of the people; even the hotel with four double doors to the street, three of which were permanently locked so that the people crowding to go through the remaining door could be more easily inspected.

If the spirit of Glasnost is going to prevail in Russia it has absolutely monumental hurdles to overcome.

And the Sterns contrasted that experience with their days in China just prior, where everyone seemed friendly and open, wanting to talk, eager to tell about the new ways of doing things, surprisingly critical about much of the past.

So we are not alone in fighting political hardening of the arteries. For better or for worse there is little we can do about the internal ethos of another country.

One reason we are all here this morning, and not someplace else, is that we are drawn to a religious point of view that encourages our growth, that doesn't try to express the truth as rigid and fixed, but rather as discoverable. We see a need to share our deepest feelings and convictions with others who may disagree totally or in part with us.

In any event, we have much to do, personally and in both our church and political institutions, to keep in touch with the real world and help them to do the same.

To recognize the process of aging is to begin to cope with it in a positive way. Let's be determined not to go the route of the dinosaurs, or the Roman Empire.

When we hear ourselves say something as though we were the Delphic Oracle, may we have the presence to say at least to ourselves, "Wait a minute! There may be a completely different explanation that hasn't even entered my head." We have to train ourselves to do that. We have to entertain, at least play around with, the most outrageous ideas. We have to see that the things we are most sure of in life do not seem all that sure to the person next to us. The most comprehensive systems are often the most out-of-date systems.

"It matters what we believe," Aunt Sophie Fahs said. "Some beliefs are like blinders, shutting off the power to choose one's own direction. Other beliefs are like gateways, opening wide vistas for exploration."

"Except you become like little children," said Jesus, "you shall not enter the kingdom."

I would like to conclude with a prayer written by the Rev. Harry Meserve.

> Let us pray:
>
> From arrogance, pompousness, and from thinking ourselves more important than we are, may some saving sense of humor liberate us.
>
> From the temptations of self-pity, the enjoyment of poor health, and the exploitation of others through our own weakness, may we have the grace to cease.
>
> From being bearers of despair, of cynicism, and of ridicule of what is young, new, and just getting started, may we be delivered.
>
> From permitting our own lack of faith to be the occasion for destroying the faith of others and for tearing down others and their efforts when we ought to build them up and support them, may we be forgiven.
>
> From making war and calling it peace, special privilege and calling it justice, indifference and calling it tolerance, pollution and calling it progress, may we be cured.
>
> From telling ourselves and others that evil is inevitable while good is impossible, may we stand corrected.
>
> God of our mixed up, tragic, aspiring, doubting and insurgent lives, help us to be as good as in our hearts we have always wanted to be. Amen.

From the Quarterly

REST IN PEACE

Fall, 1989

Truth isn't *always* stranger than fiction, but on occasion it *does* surpass anything we could invent.

This past August 9, Polly and I came home late and found a message on our answering machine. It asked me to return a call from the police chief of Oxford, Michigan. I called him the next morning.

In the meantime, some of my nighttime hours were spent wondering why I was hearing from a sleepy town forty miles north of Detroit, which I hadn't visited in about fifty years. And why from the police?

I remembered Oxford as the place we visited as a family once a year on Memorial Day when my sister and I were small children. We watched the veterans' parade, thrilled to the band music, heard the rifle salute in the cemetery, and put flowers in the mausoleum of my father's grandparents, Silas and Sarah Hovey.

I remembered that we once had very distant relatives in the town. If any remained, I had had no contact with them in half a century. Was one of them now in trouble? Had one of them died and left me a vast inheritance nobody suspected was there?

The next day I heard the real story. The mausoleum that housed my great-grandparents' remains had been broken into a month before, my great-grandmother's casket had been opened, and her skull had been stolen. The discovery of the vandalism had made sensational headlines in the Oxford newspaper. But no relatives of the Hoveys were known to exist.

The missing skull had subsequently been located as the result of an automobile accident a few days later. A young man was seen running from the accident, the skull was found in a paper bag at the scene, and so far it had been impossible to tie the man to the mausoleum break-in.

My sister, who lives in Rye, New York, and I were eventually located, also by accident, it seems. A copy of the Oxford newspaper, with its blaring headline, reached a ninety-year-old former resident of Oxford, living in California. He read the story and thought he knew someone distantly related to the Hoveys. It was my third cousin, who vaguely knew that the great-grandchildren were in the New York City area. He located us and informed the police of our whereabouts.

The upshot of this weird story is that Oakland County, Michigan, has restored the grave and mausoleum, with Sarah Hovey's missing parts returned, at no cost to the Hovey descendants. At the suggestion of the undertaker (the same man who buried her fifty-four years ago!) the mausoleum was "permanently and irrevocably sealed." Whether this was done by burying it in concrete, as was the nuclear plant in Chernoble, I do not know, and I probably will not go to Oxford to find out.

Meanwhile, I've had time to think more about the customs that have grown up to help us with the very real tragedy of death. In my great-grandparents' day, if one could possibly afford a mausoleum at a cemetery, that is what one did. Could any of us in the mid-1930s have anticipated the wild events surrounding Grandma Hovey's remains in 1989? No more, surely, than the Pharaohs pictured their pyramids being plundered and emptied. Could a stronger argument be made for cremation?

I've also had time to think some more about my great-grandmother, whom I do remember. At the age of eighty-nine she was very ill but also a very dominating woman. My sister and I feared the weekly trip we had to make up the stairs at my grandparents' house to her bedside to "pay our respects." But I suspect she loved us in her rather gruff way.

And I do owe her for one eighth of my gene pool!

May she rest (at last, and permanently and irrevocably) in peace!

Birthday Party for a Hundred-Year-Old

Spring, 1989

The year was 1970, the year Polly and I were married. We were surprised to be invited to a birthday party for a woman we had never met, who was turning a hundred years old.

If your mind has drifted to the image of a nursing home and a toothless old lady in a wheelchair, put that image away.

This was in the Grand Ballroom of the Plaza Hotel. The woman was Nanny Politzer, a life-long activist and member of the Ethical Culture Society, founder of the Encampment for Citizenship, a friend of presidents, a dear friend of Eleanor Roosevelt, and well known to all of New York City's politicians.

Seven hundred people were invited to her party. Some who arrived late or without tickets found they couldn't get in and were left standing on the sidewalks of New York.

The rest of us formed a line and walked past Nanny Politzer, who was seated in a chair and had something very personal to say to each of her seven hundred guests. Not that she could have recognized them all—she couldn't have known who we were, for example. But I'll never forget her warm, unhurried chat with us that made us feel that our being at her party was a source of pleasure for her.

From the line we went into the ballroom, with seating at tables for seven hundred. I have a vivid recollection of the several balconies packed solidly with her grandchildren, great-grandchildren and great-great-grandchildren, fifty-seven in all, if I remember correctly, banked like flowers, looking down on the proceedings below.

Following dinner there was a birthday cake, with a hundred candles, which a cortege of great-great-grandchildren helped her to blow out. Then, some short speeches by congressmen and others. Finally the major address of the evening.

You guessed it! Delivered by Nanny Politzer herself! She spoke for twenty minutes, standing throughout, without notes, in a clear voice, and with absolute clarity of thought. Only at one point did her memory falter. She recovered, and added sheepishly, "That's what happens when you get to be a hundred."

Incidentally, the reason we were at the party in the first place was that we had been invited by Nanny Politzer's younger sister, Lucille Kohn, whom we *did* know. We saw little of Lucille that night because she had staged the entire affair and was behind the scenes throughout the party, making sure that everything ran smoothly. Lucille, at the time, was a mere *eighty-four!*

A Weekend in My Life
(Or "How Clothes Help to Make the Clergyperson")

Fall, 1989

Friday, May 15

6:00 a.m. Puts on a dark blue suit for two late afternoon wedding rehearsals.

7:30 a.m. Takes bus to his financial counseling business in Florham, Park, N.J. Has his violin with him because he has over-scheduled his day and has no time to go home to get his violin before his concert tonight. Fortunately, has a black suit hanging in the church and he puts a bow tie in his pocket before heading to Jersey.

2:00 p.m. Arrives back at All Souls and locks up the violin.

2:30 p.m. Sees a parishioner in New York Hospital.

5:00 p.m. Has first wedding rehearsal, at the Carlyle Hotel, still in the blue suit.

6:15 p.m. Polly arrives from her office to assist with second wedding rehearsal, at All Souls. Then a quick change into the black suit and bow tie.

7:50 p.m. Arrives at the concert just in time to tune up.

Questions for study:

1. Where is the blue suit now?
2. The violin?
3. The bow tie?
4. What happened to dinner?

Saturday, May 16

9:00 a.m. Studies closely the four wedding services he will do today and tomorrow.

1:00 p.m. Dons the tuxedo that will be needed at third wedding reception today.

1:30 p.m. Arrives with Polly at All Souls and changes to the blue suit for weddings one and two.

2:30 p.m. Wedding number one in the chapel.

4:30 p.m. Wedding number two in the main church.

5:30 p.m. Puts in appearance with Polly at the second wedding reception a block away.

6:30 p.m. Returns to the church, switches to the tux and grabs the ministerial robe. Meanwhile, Polly changes to the cocktail dress she carried to church earlier.

7:30 p.m. Wedding number three and reception at the Carlyle Hotel.

8:30 p.m. We cut out to attend a celebration for Wally Klauss, the church organist, apologizing there for appearing so formal.

Questions for study:

1. Where is the blue suit now?
2. The black suit?
3. The bow tie?
4. The violin?

Sunday, May 17

8:00 a.m. Arrives at All Souls to double-check maintenance and name tags, in the black suit.

10:00 a.m. Wedding number four at the United Nations Chapel, with robe.

10:45 a.m. Back to All Souls for the morning service.

1:00 p.m. Attends party for Mary-Ella Holst.

2:30 p.m. Changes back to the blue suit so the black one will be available again at the church.

3:30 p.m. Arrives at the wrong hospital with flowers for a parishioner.

4:00 p.m. Arrives at the right hospital and has a nice visit.

5:30 p.m. Arrives home and begins answering messages from the answering machine and planning the next week.

Questions for study:

1. What happened to the bow tie?

Poems

THE SUNDAY BEFORE CHRISTMAS
(or A Visit from Just About Everybody)

Revised, December, 1993

'Twas the Sunday before Christmas, and all through the church
Every creature was stirring, one needn't to search.
The hymnbooks were placed in their pew racks with care
In hopes the congregation soon would be there.
Some children were home, getting out of their beds,
While visions of coffeecake danced in their heads.

And Forrest in his vestments and Galen in blue
Had just picked their readings, both Biblical and new,
When out on the street there arose such a clatter,
I sprang from my desk to see what was the matter.
Away to the lobby I flew, feeling queasy,
Tore open the double doors; that wasn't so easy!

The sun on the asphalt and trash overflow
Gave a harsh luster of midday to objects below.
When what to my wondering eyes should appear,
But a host of people coming to have their pictures taken for the
    new directory that comes out next year.
Then, a smiling young clergyman, lively and quick.
I knew that Forrest Church was out doing his 'schtick.'

More rapid than coursers his congregants came,
And he whistled and shouted, and called them by name:
"Now Abbot! Now, Phillips! Now, Condliffes! Now, Speyer!
On, Moffat! On, Halbergs! On, Bechman and Meyer!"
To the top of the steps, through the vestibule too
The folks kept on coming, to fill every pew.

Then in a twinkling I heard from on high
The peal of the organ, and the heavens reply.
As I drew in my head and was turning around,
Down the main aisle came the choir with a bound.
They were dressed all in red from their head to their toe,
And they sang like the angels of centuries ago.

Up to the pulpit our leader arose,
Discarding a baseball cap. (Mets, I suppose.)
A wink of his eye and a nod of his head
Soon gave us to know we had nothing to dread.
He spake many words (it's part of his work)
And filled all our noggins, then turned with a jerk.

We sang one more carol, a glorious song.
Then laying his arm out over the throng,
He gave us his blessing, a churchly dismissal,
And away people fled like the down of a thistle.
But I heard them exclaim as they went out of view,
"Happy Christmas to all, and a good New Year's too!

      With apologies to Clement Moore and
          lovers of poetry everywhere.

THE MODERN UNITARIAN
(with apologies to W. S. Gilbert)

September 6, 1992

I am the very model of a modern Unitarian.
I've information worldwide, both cultured and barbarian;
I memorize *The New York Times* and magazines historical,
And list the major world events in order categorical;
I'm very well acquainted, too, with matters theological,
I understand religion, both revealed and pedagogical;

About the films and theater I'm teeming with a lot of news,
While many things I talk about are gathered out of book reviews.
I'm very good at balancing a host of views contrarian,
I know where all the churches are, from Brooklyn First to
    Darien.
In short, in matters worldwide, both cultured and barbarian,
I am the very model of a modern Unitarian.

I know religious history from Babylon to Khomenei,
I've written much that's noted for incomprehensibility;
My taste for social justice borders on the bit fanatical,
My zest for free expression has been rated as dogmatical.
I understand the greatest works of art in Steen's portfolio,
I know the Hallelujah parts in Handel's oratorio;

Then I can lecture easily on Rubik's mathematica,
And list the known diseases from the measles to sciatica;
And I can tell the fine points of the Battle of Thermopolae,
And help the budding chess hound in a gambit get "the drop"
    thereby.
In short, in matters worldwide, both cultured and barbarian,
I am the very model of the modern Unitarian.

In fact, when I know what is meant by *Kairos* and *dichotomy,*
When I can tell at sight a lobster claw from a lobotomy,
And when I know precisely what is meant by esoterica,
When such affairs I look askance as Pageants Miss America,
When I have learnt more word play than Bill Buckley in a
 punnery,
When I know more of tactics than a novice in a nunnery,

In short, when I've a smattering of what it takes to get a laugh,
You'll say, "Let's get the crazy Unitary rector's autograph."
For my academic knowledge, though I'm plucky and adventury,
Has only been brought down to the beginning of the century.
But still in learning worldwide, both cultured and barbarian,
I am the very model of a modern Unitarian.

Annual Report to the Congregation

February 3, 1998

Until I read the agenda tonight I wasn't sure whether a minister emeritus was expected to speak at an annual meeting or not, so I have been scratching something on my notes at the back of the room. I did notice that ministers are advised to give *brief* reports, so mine will be brief.

First, I want to thank you again for the honor you bestowed on me last September.

Second, I want to leave some advice with you as we set out in this exciting capital campaign year. Because there are so many reports to be given tonight, I thought I'd try to say everything worth saying in just two words. Here they are.

Work hard! Play fair! Look ahead! Keep smiling!

Act natural, avoid cliches, stay warm, keep cool, live free, come clean, do justice, don't smoke, avoid complications, fight crime, question authority, get married, stay married, pursue learning, entertain angels, don't overdo, don't underdo, judge not, keep focused, lose weight, pop corn, respect nature, try harder, think big, mend fences, donate organs, welcome strangers, pay bills, pay pledges, pay attention, love mercy, make whoopee, provide shelter, sow seeds, alter egos, consider lilies, cultivate beauty, keep hope, stand fast, grow up, age slowly, love God, suffer idiots, say prayers, stay well.

Pardon me,

Thank you!

And

THE DAY THE RUSSIANS CAME
by The Rev. Richard Leonard

August 16, 1990

Polly and I have traveled a great deal, and I consider myself quite experienced in an airport setting. When Bruce Clear, our Unitarian Universalist minister in Vancouver, Washington, telephoned with his unusual problem, the need to transfer fourteen Russians whose knowledge of English was minimal or nonexistent, between two airplanes at Kennedy Airport, I was interested both from a humanitarian point of view and for the challenge it would present. I volunteered to personally "make it happen."

The problem was this: twelve fifteen- to eighteen-year-old Russian youngsters, accompanied by two adults, all from Sakhalin Island in the USSR, were scheduled to arrive at Kennedy about 3 p.m. on August 15, 1990. They would be coming via Aeroflot, the Russian airline. They were scheduled to depart for Portland, Oregon, at 5:30 p.m., via Delta Airlines, with a change of planes in Salt Lake City. Baggage would need to be routed directly to Portland.

If Aeroflot were on time and the group passed through customs easily, two and a half hours seemed like plenty of time to get them from one terminal to another by way of the bus system that links the terminals. "What if Aeroflot is very late and we miss the connection with Delta?" I had asked Vicki Colclazier, who had made the arrangements in Vancouver on behalf of her church.

"Delta has agreed to put them up overnight at Kennedy and fly them out the next day," she replied. Vicki had their airline tickets for the U.S. portion of the trip; she would express them overnight to me.

Two days later, armed with fourteen tickets (worth about $5,100, I realized later), I took the Carey bus to Kennedy in plenty of time. (The only secret to air travel is starting for the airport as close to a full day ahead of time as one can comfortably manage!)

By 1 p.m. I was at the Delta desk, which turned out to be in Pan Am's "A" Terminal. Pan Am had an A and B Terminal at Kennedy, I discovered, adjacent to each other, but still with quite a bit of real estate between them.

The Delta operation looked minuscule, with only one desk open and apparently a scant four flights scheduled to leave all afternoon, including ours at 5:30 p.m. to Salt Lake City.

The Delta ticket representative was engaged in a complex conversation with the one customer on the scene. When a second Delta employee emerged, a matronly woman who looked bored with the world, I asked her if she could get a Delta supervisor for me because I was holding fourteen Delta tickets.

"In a few minutes, when I get back," she replied.

A few minutes later she returned, and again with boredom written all over her face, she allowed that she would hear my situation. I sketched it out, she jotted down a few notes, but curiously, in pencil on the back of a dark blue Delta folder so that I could not see anything legible being recorded. Then I tossed out the hook: "I understand that if Aeroflot is late and these people miss their connection, Delta has agreed to put them up overnight at the airport." She mumbled something, picked up the phone and delivered the news that there was no such record with them. However, she took the name and telephone number of Vicki in Vancouver, and said she would check it out.

"Let's see if Aeroflot is on time," she volunteered helpfully. I had brought Aeroflot's 800 number. "They are scheduled to land at 2:40," was the word. That was good news! It gave us a bigger margin for the connection, and made discussion of an overnight at the airport seem academic. I thanked her.

Having stood on the spot where my charges would present their tickets, I left on foot for the International Arrivals Building nearby, where I was sure Areoflot would arrive. Many questions later, in the various national airlines offices, I was convinced that Aeroflot would arrive at one of the two Pan Am terminals. I returned to the original area happy that we would apparently not need to use the bus system that connects the terminals in the airport.

But, on a less happy note, it seemed that Aeroflot would land at Pan Am Terminal B, and my Russians would leave from Delta in Pan Am Terminal A. A moving walkway connected the two buildings, but was tied to Pan Am B at the third floor, and that was reachable only from the customs exit on the first floor by two slow elevators, already being over-used as a late afternoon crowd was developing. I made a walking round trip between the two buildings, finding the shorter of two possible routes in case we had to forget the elevators and push their luggage at street level.

I was now ready, at 2:30 p.m., confident that the situation was well in hand. I had brought a somewhat crude but easily readable sign: UNITARIAN CHURCH, VANCOUVER, WASHINGTON. Surely one of the fourteen would recognize at least one of the four words as relating to them, and we would make the connection as they came out of customs. By 2:55 p.m. we knew the plane had landed.

By 3:15 p.m. they had not come through, or by 3:30. But I knew customs would take awhile. I thoroughly enjoyed seeing the reunions taking place as people emerged with their luggage, walked through a narrow path between now hundreds of people hoping to make identifications, and in many cases, fell into someone's arms with weeping, kissing, and laughing, an altogether moving scene.

3:45 p.m. Still no sign of my group. One group of young people has come out, which I was sure was mine. But they looked at my sign, passed right by, and one said in perfect English, "Your sign is upside down!" As I turned the sign right-side up, I thought, "Definitely not my group," and I took a firmer grip on my leather pouch with its fourteen precious tickets.

4 p.m. Getting tired of holding the sign. Getting claustrophobic as the crowd presses in more and more. Getting nervous over the failure of my people to appear. But we still have one and a half hours, and we are only next door to our ultimate destination. Now I am hearing conflicting rumors: Everyone on Flight 031 has come through! Almost nobody on Flight 031 has come through! Four big planes are unloading at the same time! There is another customs area where some people have come out!

4:15 p.m. Half of our time is gone. Surely they will appear at any moment now. The stream of people pouring out of customs now is increasing, and so is the crowd receiving them. Could they walk right past me?

4:30 p.m. Decision-making time. They could have gotten past me or even been escorted by a different route to Delta, which would be fine except I am holding all of their tickets. If I go to Delta with their tickets, I may miss them here and never connect up with them. If I stay here, they may get to Delta without their tickets.

4:40 p.m. I decide to run to Delta and back as fast as I can, leaving the tickets if Delta will hold them. I ask a man if he will hold my sign for five minutes. "Hell no!' he says. "I'm expecting an eighty-year-old man!" Don't count on anyone else to help, I tell myself. For the first time I begin to wonder why I came on this mission alone.

4:45 p.m. I race to Delta as fast as my sixty-three-year-old legs (that once played basketball) will take me, dodging a car here and there on the not-overly-safe but surely the shortest route.

"I have fourteen people coming from Aeroflot to your 5:30 plane! Will you hold these tickets?" "Okay," says the person at the ticket counter. I plunk down $5,100 worth of tickets and race back out at the same speed that I came in, but also noting that suddenly Delta is just as busy as Pan Am, with long lines and one person complaining, "I've been in this line for half an hour!" When I get my people to Delta, will I find impossible confusion?

4:50 p.m. Back at customs in the other building. The confusion is worse. I must watch people coming out of customs in a steady stream, but also scan areas where my troop might have collected in the last five minutes, perhaps distraught that they have not been met. Are they at the elevators, which I can't see and which are swamped with people?

4:55 p.m. I must try to telephone Delta and tell them what is happening. I find a telephone in view of the customs exit. It is also necessary to hold the sign up even as I dial, because one or more people may now be frantically looking for it. I have three quarters in my pocket. (I almost always, by design, have at least three quarters in my pocket for telephone calls on the streets of New York—this time I have exactly three, no more, no less.) The first Delta number I try costs me one quarter—the message is on tape, is too complicated, and can't be figured out in the sea of voices around me. I try a different Delta number, holding the sign at the same time. The message is that one must first deposit a quarter to make that call. "BUT I HAVE ALREADY DEPOSITED A QUARTER!" I want to shout at the mechanical voice. Sure enough, when I have hung up, the quarter does not come back. I look at the last quarter, and on a hunch, repeat exactly what I had done on the previous call.

This time a charming, live voice answers on the other end, "Delta Airlines, may I help you?" I try to explain the situation in about three sentences, and ask if she can alert the Delta desk at Kennedy to the fact that fourteen Russian passengers should be arriving at their gate very soon now. She says she will try.

5:05 p.m. Checking areas where they might have collected, while keeping an eye on the never-ending stream of arrivals.

5:10 p.m. Checking areas where they might have collected, while watching the unending stream.

5:15 p.m. Watching the steady stream of Mexicans, Asians, families with small children, elderly couples, most undoubtedly coming from other planes than Aeroflot SU 031.

5:20 p.m. We're losing it! Where will we put them for the night if Delta won't do it? How would I get the group to Manhattan, and where would I take them?

5:25 p.m. We've lost it! I couldn't get them to the next building in time if they walked out of customs right now. A bright flash of an idea! Since that is the case, I should abandon hope here, race to the next building and just possibly make a connection between the people and their tickets at the last moment. I take two running steps for the door. Stop, you idiot! You're too late for that. The odds are about as good that they come now through customs. I take two slower steps back toward customs.

What is this? A man seems to recognize my sign. There are young people behind him. They are holding lots of luggage, but I don't see any luggage carts. The man is tired, and disgusted with their ordeal in customs, but a flicker of hope is being kindled.

"We may still make it," I announce, more to myself than to them. I gesture. "Can your people carry their things? We'll run!" The answer seems to be affirmative. I gesture and head for the door. They are following. I glance at my watch. It is 5:25!

At the street I break into a run, the man running behind me. The others seem to be coming in single file. Now I am on a route I know only too well, sometimes on a sidewalk, sometimes in the street. Surely cars will stop at this unusual sight. I glance over my shoulder and gesture to the man toward the building we are heading for. The sight behind me is remarkable—fourteen people running in single file with their luggage, the line stretching farther and farther, but each one keeping in touch with the person ahead. I increase my speed; I must be there by 5:30.

I run up the sidewalk into Pan Am A and continue running, not a short distance, to the Delta desk. "They're coming." I shout.

"The Russians?"

"Yes, the group from Aeroflot."
"Do you see them?"
"Yes they are coming through the door!"
I look back. They are *not* coming through the door.
I run back to the main doors and look. They have collected by a lamppost below. They have lost me. "Up here! Up here!" They spot me, grab their bags, and head in my direction.
I run back to the desk. "They're coming! Through the front door, now!" They *are* coming!
Now the desk is alive, with three persons working on fourteen tickets and baggage checks. Some bags are going in the cabin, some are being checked to Portland. We can't find one ticket; there are only thirteen. After search through all the papers, we come up with the 14th. A Delta representative has all their boarding passes together. Now we run for Gate 34, some starting in one direction, some in another, but we bring the stream together at the gate and I realize that they are going to go aboard.
But I have not even seen their faces, much less said, "Hello," or "Welcome to our country!" I must make some effort at cordiality.
As the first young man starts to go past me, I indicate a handshake. He puts his bag down, shakes my hand vigorously with a smile, and I say "Good luck!" The second teenager puts her bag down, shakes my hand with a smile, and I say, "Good luck!" The third. I will do it to all, including the adults. All are grinning; they have interesting faces.
I would have liked to tell them that Polly and I were in Russia two years ago. I would have liked to give them the aerial-view postcard of Manhattan that I had bought leisurely at 1:15, and pointed out where we live and work. I would have liked to try to communicate to them that chess is my favorite game, and that in 1979 I had the pleasure of playing their world champion Anatoly Karpov and their runner-up expatriate Viktor Korchnoi. I am settling for fourteen "Good lucks!" None says "Thank you," which means they don't know what "Good luck!" means. And I can't remember a suitable word of Russian.

They are gone, down the passageway to Delta Flight 1425 to Salt Lake City. I hope someone is looking out for them in Salt Lake City for the transfer to the Portland flight. But they are both Delta planes, and it should be easy.

As I walk away from the passageway, I realize I haven't run as much in the last fifteen years. The old ticker seems to be going fine, though. I do feel emotionally drained. Is there anything I missed, or did wrong, that I should be checking on? I go through the many ticket folders and papers in my pouch.

My God! I've got all their tickets for the Salt Lake City to Portland flight! How did *that* happen? They are all loose in a single folder, apparently separated by the Delta people! I run back to the gate. The passageway is open and there is no one to stop me, so I run down the passageway to the plane. Its door is open and the first officer has his hand on the handle.

"Wait I've got all their tickets for Salt Lake City to Portland!" I describe the man, recently aboard, who should get the tickets. We laugh and I head back up the tube. Flight 1425 is on its way, with fourteen Russians who have been given a very interesting impression of "the other great superpower," an endless ordeal in customs and then a race with their luggage across part of the airport. I wonder what they are saying to each other, in Russian, on the plane now.

That evening, when we are home and I've told my story to Polly, I once again go through the flotsam and jetsam that I've brought back from the airport. This time I find I have all of their return-trip tickets from Portland to New York, value: $2,600. I telephone to Vancouver, Washington, and tell them not to worry—the tickets will be mailed express tomorrow.

And they were. Now, what other stone did I leave unturned?

THE DAY THE RUSSIANS WENT HOME
by The Rev. Bruce Clear

September 4, 1990

We thought about asking Dick Leonard again for some help, but decided we wouldn't need him. Little did we know at the time that we would need a U.S. senator, two congressional representatives (one being the speaker of the House, third in line of succession to the president), *The Atlanta Constitution*, the U. S. State Department, the Soviet Embassy, the FAA, and maybe even the New York City Police Department. We bypassed George Bush, since he seemed preoccupied with Saddam Hussein and the sand trap of the ninth hole at the Kennebunkport Country Club. And, as I say, we did not need the good offices of Dick Leonard after all.

The Rev. Richard Leonard is a minister of All Souls Church in New York. In this narrative, "we" refers to nine families who sent eleven of our teenagers to the Soviet Union earlier in the summer. For the last two weeks, we and three other families had been hosting twelve Soviet children and two adult escorts in our homes. These students were from the Soviet families that hosted our kids the previous month.

When the Soviet children came to the United States, we had carefully planned a stayover in Washington, D.C., for them, but a sudden change of plans sent them through New York with a brief change of airplanes at Kennedy International.

Seven of our nine families are from the Unitarian Church of Vancouver, where I am minister. In desperation, I called All Souls in New York to find someone who might be able to meet the Soviet children and their two adult escorts and guide them from one plane to the next. Dick Leonard willingly responded to our request with skill and grace, and though his experience at Kennedy was a real cliff-hanger, all's well that ended well and the Soviets arrived on schedule.

They were here for two wonderful weeks in our homes. Each day was full, as the combined group of kids and parents visited sights from morning to night and ended each night with a Soviet-American teenage party lasting till 11 p.m. The bonding between the Americans—children and parents—and the Soviet children was spectacular. I would love to tell you about the charming and beautiful Olga who stayed in our home, but that would distract me from the point of this essay. Let it be said, though, that the affection between these groups was so strong that we knew our final moments at the airport would be heartrending and tearful.

The return itinerary was for the Soviet group to fly Delta airlines from Portland, Oregon, through Salt Lake City to Kennedy in New York. At Kennedy they would have over an hour and a half to make a connection with a joint Pan Am and Aeroflot flight to Moscow. The problem at the time of their arrival had been a two-hour wait at U.S. customs. That was not to be a factor in their leaving, so we decided not to bother Dick Leonard about this one. He'd had enough adventures at Kennedy International.

The night before their departure we had a tearful closing ceremony at the church, and went home to finish packing to be ready for a pre-dawn, 4 a.m. rendezvous at the airport. Delta flight 1262 was to leave for Salt Lake City at 5:25 a.m. If other families were like mine, we were up past midnight, packing, exchanging gifts, saying goodbye. We awoke again at 3 a.m. Sleep was brief.

We gathered in the dark at 4 a.m. at the airport and organized ourselves, processed tickets, took many final pictures, and proceeded to the gate. The Soviet and American children formed a circle, and the Soviets sang a wonderful song. There were more tears. It was about 5:10 and they would be boarding soon. A delay was announced.

At 5:25 a.m.—the scheduled departure time—a Delta agent came over and in a casual, "Oh, by the way" attitude announced that the flight was canceled due to some mechanical problem on the plane. Panic did not set in at first. We had plenty of time for Delta to find another flight to New York, and besides, all were relieved that the final goodbye was postponed. Anyway, Delta assured us that they would find a way. Don't worry.

A half hour passed, and our relief at having extra time together began to transform into anxiety. Are they going to get to New York on time? To understand the problem that affected the rest of our day, one must be aware of the following axiom: People who miss their Aeroflot flight may have lost any chance of getting any flight. Aeroflot gives no guarantees about missed connections. This principle was verified by both our Soviet friends and American friends who had flown on Aeroflot. That was reason for anxiety.

If they missed the New York connection, they could be stuck in New York for days, maybe weeks, maybe months, who knows? But there was an even more complex problem. These children were from Sakhalin Island on the Pacific coast of the Soviet Union, thousands of miles from Moscow. Even if they missed their connection in New York and caught the Pan Am/Aeroflot flight to Moscow the following day, they would also miss their Aeroflot connection *within* the USSR, and they would be stuck in Moscow with possibly worthless tickets.

We tried to explain this problem to Delta. They didn't care. "Our responsibility is to get you to New York, and we will do that," was their mantra. We told them they would have to house these kids in New York or Moscow for months in order to make up for their mistake. They weren't impressed.

Like many airlines, Delta hires employees whose primary function is to mollify disgruntled customers. They are instructed, I believe, to do everything in their power to prevent customers from talking directly to the Individual Who Can Actually Do Something About the Problem. "We're doing everything we can," is tattooed on the forehead of these employees.

But this wasn't good enough for a group of American parents who had spent two weeks falling in love with these delightful Soviet children who were now being sent by Delta into the black hole of corporate apathy. We would do whatever had to be done to protect (now) *our* Soviet children! We told them to charter a special plane, hire a corporate jet, but get them to New York on time! They didn't care.

The parents dispersed in different directions. One went to the phones to call Delta's corporate headquarters and eventually talked with a high level manager in their San Francisco office. Other parents stormed the central offices of the Portland airport. Other parents remained at the counter, being as headstrong and obnoxious as possible to the employees whose job it is to prevent customers from speaking directly to the Individual Who Can Actually Do Something About The Problem.

I went to the phone to call the Washington, D.C., office of Congresswoman Jolene Unsoeld (known affectionately by her supporters as simply "Jolene"). I explained the complicated situation, in the course of which I informed Jolene's staffer that all the parents were strong Jolene supporters. (This may have been an exaggeration. I was familiar with the political leanings of most of the parents involved, but not all. But it was true enough to fudge on the remainder.) Could Jolene's office contact someone in the State Department, maybe, who could put pressure on Delta or Aeroflot? "Susan" said she'd get right on it, and she did.

We waited. At about 6:45 a.m., the Individual Who Can Actually Do Something About The Problem appeared from the cave behind the Delta ticket counter. It seems the pressure from the parents who scattered to get help scared him out. But he came with bad news.

"There are no flights to get you to New York on time," he said. "However, there is a plane leaving at 7 a.m. for Atlanta, and a transfer in Atlanta could get you to New York by 5:35 p.m." There's hope. "But the Pan Am/Aeroflot flight to Moscow is scheduled to depart at 5:25." No hope. "But weather conditions predict backups all day at Kennedy, and there is a chance the Pan Am/Aeroflot flight is delayed, by maybe an hour." Hope. "But the Delta flight from Atlanta doesn't land at Kennedy, it lands at LaGuardia." No hope. "But Delta will have a bus ready to shuttle them from LaGuardia to Kennedy, and maybe if the Pan Am/Aeroflot flight is delayed enough, and maybe if the Delta from Atlanta is ahead of schedule, *maybe* they could make it." Slim hope, but hope.

We confer with the two Soviet adults, and decide to try it. We've got less than ten minutes to get to the gate for the 7 a.m. to Atlanta. As we rush down the terminal, I hear my name paged on the loud speaker. When I pick up the paging phone, I'm told to call Jolene Unsoeld's office at a particular phone number. Jolene will have to wait, I think to myself. Right now I must say goodbye to the Soviet students.

At the gate, there are hugs and tears but there is no real time to say all the things we want to say. Americans and Soviets cannot let go of each other. A Delta voice comes over the intercom, sounding like a frustrated school teacher with an unruly class: "You American host families must move away from the Russian students so they can make their connection in Atlanta." Pause. Then: "Move away now! They must board now!" A couple of Soviet kids will not go. Crying and screaming, they are literally pulled into the tube. They are gone from our sight, finally. Sadly.

But the day's work has just begun for the American host families. We must make sure they do not get stranded in New York or Moscow. Remember the axiom: If Aeroflot connections are missed, either in New York or Moscow, the tickets become worthless.

We make a beeline to the Delta ticket booth and talk again with the Individual Who Can Actually Do Something About The Problem. We plead that the Pan Am/Aeroflot flight in New York must be delayed until the students arrive. He says that Delta will request it, but Pan Am will probably refuse.

Before leaving the airport, I call Jolene's office again, and explain what has happened. They have been talking with the State Department, but now there is one single objective: to persuade Pan Am to hold its Aeroflot flight in New York. The American families go home to spend the day on the phone.

Someone has suggested contacting Washington Senator Brock Adams, who had made transportation his area of expertise. From home, I call Adams' office, and they say they will work on it. A few minutes later, Susan from Jolene's office calls to say they have heard Adams has been contacted, and maybe the two offices can be working together. (They did.)

Another parent calls the Federal Aviation Administration and finds a surprisingly sympathetic response. It seems there is something called the Emergency Transportation Agency and there is a possibility that we can get a helicopter at LaGuardia to carry the Soviets to make their connection at Kennedy. If not, they can at least have a police escort for their Delta bus between airports.

Another host family calls Congressman Tom Foley's office. Foley is not from our district, but he is from Washington State, and he is, after all, speaker of the House. This turns out to be a very fortunate call. Someone in Foley's office is closely connected to the Soviet Embassy. The embassy is contacted, and Foley's office receives word that if the students miss their connection in New York, the Soviet embassy will guarantee an Aeroflot flight to Moscow, and connecting flights from Moscow to Sakhalin. This is an encouraging word, but from experience we know such a guarantee is somewhat less than a hundred percent certain.

Another parent has a brilliant idea. Delta is headquartered in Atlanta. Maybe the local newspaper, *The Atlanta Constitution*, one of the best major papers in the country, would be interested in this story and help pressure Delta to act. With a cellphone call, she learns that the paper is interested. We think that if Delta doesn't care about congressional pressure, surely they will be nervous about bad press coverage. Our parent says to the reporter:

"Maybe you can ask Delta if they are willing to pay for hotel lodging for these students in New York or Moscow for the next few months while they are waiting for Aeroflot tickets." The reporter promises to contact Delta, Adams, Foley, the FAA, everyone. Sounds good.

[As an aside, there is some evidence and speculation that Delta intentionally screwed up on this one. Rumor: Our plane to Salt Lake City had not been canceled due to mechanical problems; it was not full enough. The only passengers were our group of fourteen and one other family of three. Rumor: Pilots can fly no more than a specified number of hours each month, and it is common for flights at Portland to be canceled in the last days of each month because pilots have used their quota of hours. "Mechanical problems" are usually cited as the reason for cancellation. Rumor: The plane had been there all night, and no one noticed this "mechanical problem" until just before departure. Rumor: The family that had been waiting with our group to go to Salt Lake City told one of our people they saw the plane, which had been at the gate for "5:25 to Salt Lake City" simply move around to another gate labeled "7 a.m. to Atlanta." This was the plane our group (and the family) eventually took. Rumor: One of our parents later contacted a travel agent friend and found there was no scheduled Delta departure from Portland to Atlanta at 7 a.m. Speculation: Did Delta cancel the flight to Salt Lake because it was underbooked or because of pilot hour problems, and then when they received pressure from congressional offices and irate parents and supervisors at headquarters, simply provide the plane to Atlanta? We passed these rumors and speculations on to the FAA and *the Atlanta Constitution.*]

We were getting by on only a few hours sleep from the night before. Phone calls were non-stop, keeping each other informed. Communication central became Vicki Colclazier's house because she has two phone lines. I stretched out on the couch, placing my cordless phone on my stomach, trying to catch a few minutes of sleep between phone calls, but wanting the phone to wake me up with more news. I assume others were in similar positions.

Congressional offices kept in touch. (Delta remained silent, of course.) We watched the clock as we figured they were landing in Atlanta, and when they were scheduled to leave Atlanta. Good news was received: the Pan Am/Areoflot flight out of Kennedy had been delayed one hour. Bad news was received: even with a helicopter waiting to transport them to Kennedy, their baggage would have to be rechecked, and the helicopter could probably not get them to Kennedy within the one-hour window of opportunity. We were discouraged. Privately, we all felt the kids would certainly enjoy the helicopter ride.

Jolene's office promised to keep us informed, and they did. The bad news eventually came: the students missed their connection to Pan Am/Aeroflot. Other news was encouraging: a promise from Delta to put them up at a hotel, with meals; a promise from Pan Am/Aeroflot that they could get to Moscow the next day; a promise from the Soviet Embassy that they would honor their Aeroflot connections to Sakhalin after arrival in Moscow.

That night there were phone calls between some of our families and the airport hotel. The Soviet kids loved the hotel and were having a good time there. The next morning, the group left the hotel early to spend the day at the airport. Twenty-four hours late, they boarded Pan Am/Aeroflot for Moscow. It was a week before we finally had contact with them on Sakhalin; their connections in Moscow worked.

One wonders what the Cold War was all about, anyway. If Ike or JFK, LBJ, or Tricky Dick had welcomed someone like fourteen-year-old Olga in their home for two weeks, I am sure they would have found a better way for countries to relate to one another than by fear and nuclear threat. If our governments had put half as much effort into understanding one another as we did in trying to protect these children we learned to love, or as the Soviet group did in being so gracious and caring toward our children, the enmity between our countries that has existed throughout my lifetime would not have been possible.

September 4, 1990
Bruce Clear, Minister

Michael Servetus Unitarian Universalist Fellowship
Vancouver, Washington

Epilogue

Astronomers estimate that there are two trillion stars in the universe for every human life on the planet earth. (That's 2,000,000,000,000!)

Biologists calculate that there is a staggering ten times as many atoms in an average human hair, each atom a universe of its own, its countless parts held mysteriously together.

Humankind walks a fragile path through those numbers, capable of warring on itself but also of creating symphonies of sublime complexity and delight, capable of putting machinery on another planet millions of miles away, but also able to destroy the very home on which life depends. Truly we are, individually and together, on a journey the full meaning of which is far beyond all but our faintest understanding. Yet, in a process that has taken perhaps fifteen billion years, the human species has developed, with minds that calculate, eyes that see, feelings that intertwine with the feelings of others, powers to attract and make love and reproduce the species, all of this outside of any conscious effort our part.

Each of us faces the fact that we are born, against incredible odds reaching back to the beginning of time, and each of us is destined to die, to rejoin the elements from which we arose, and to make way for our descendants. It is an unfolding drama that gives rise to our search for meaning, and the existence of philosophy and the world religions.

The sermons and other writings that I have collected in this book were the products of my ministry in All Souls Church between 1981 and 2000. In each I do my best to avoid the common fallacy of defining the "meaning of life" for the human race, or even for myself as an individual. Instead, as I have throughout my ministry, I delight in pointing out the unusual events that challenge my own and others' interpretations of life's meanings. I continue to believe that GROWTH, our ability to change and adapt, is as important as taking stands. My writings, I believe, reflect my concern for new frontiers, the unlearning of old truths in favor of new truths, helping others to find new liberating truths for their lives.

Looking back over fifty-four years of ministry, two public events outweigh all others in their influence on me. The first was being part of the civil rights movement in Selma in 1965 and hearing the stories of oppression that were told by the citizens of Dallas County, Alabama, many of which are recorded in my companion book "Call to Selma: Eighteen Days of Witness."

The other event that has challenged my outlook on life and led me to search for new meaning was the 9/11 terrorist attack on America. Without ignoring other violent acts (our own included) the destruction of the World Trade Towers and the attack on the Pentagon illustrated clearly what a small group of people, with utter contempt for humans not sharing their beliefs, could do with the powers we all have in hand. To have walked, as I did, directly under the American Airlines Flight 11 as it came down Park Avenue headed for the World Trade Center that morning, without recognizing its mission or the sheer panic that must at that moment have engulfed its passengers, is to have been marked for life.

From time to time life brings us almost unbearable pain, and a search for meaning. Fortunately, it also brings joy and healing and hope. Martin Luther King, Jr., and many who preceded him, dreamed of a world community where wars were a thing of the past, where people treated each other as brothers and sisters, where one's race had no bearing on one's place in society, where countries lived by the rule of law, not by might.

Just as we are poised between a measureless universe and the adventures of uncountable atoms, so we hover between the idealism of a Dr. King and the nihilism of the religious fanatic. The sermons in this book all predate the events of September 11. Even now to me they reflect a different era, and a slightly different author, now wiser and older.

My fondest hope (and we humans ARE given to hope) is that the idealism of Dr. King, and before him of Jesus, Gandhi, Eleanor Roosevelt, Dag Hammarskold, Adlai Stevenson, Wendell Willkie, and so many others, will pull us back from the precipice and give us more time to enjoy our precious life together. We can, and must, be active partners in that endeavor.

Acknowledgements

Sincere thanks are due to the following individuals and organizations for permission to quote from material on which they hold copyrights:

Page 11: "Human Family," copyright © 1990 by Maya Angelou, from "I SHALL NOT BE MOVED," by Maya Angelou. Used by permission of Random House.

Page 12: Permission to reprint from the Rev. Marjorie Bowens-Wheatley, minister of the Unitarian Universalist Church of Tampa, Florida.

Page 15: Copyright © 1999 by *The New York Times* Co. Reprinted with permission.

Page 19: Permission from Sarah Flynn, from her "Credo," delivered as a junior high to the congregation of All Souls Church in New York on April 19, 1998.

Page 29: "A Considerable Speck (Microscopic)" from THE POETRY OF ROBERT FROST edited by Edward Connery Lathem. Copyright 1942 by Robert Frost, copyright 1970 by Lesley Frost Ballantine, copyright 1969 by Henry Holt and Company. Reprinted by permission of Henry Holt and Company, LLC.

Page 52: From A HISTORY OF THE ARAB PEOPLE, by Albert Hourani. Permission from Faber & Faber, Ltd., publishers, 3 Queen Square, London, U.K. WC IN 3 AU.

Page 60: "I Continually Think of Those," copyright 1934 and renewed 1964 by Stephen Spender, from COLLECTED POEMS 1928–1985, by Stephen Spender. Used by permission of Random House.

Page 68: Permission by Mrs. Paul Carnes. She writes, "I do remember, vividly, those words of Paul's from I believe a 'STRICTLY PERSONAL' column he usually wrote for our church's newsletter. It was written in 1964 the week that he learned that his slow recovery from a bout of the flu might be more serious than he wanted to believe." (Paul died of lymphoma in 1979 while serving as president of the Unitarian Universalist Association, at the age of fifty-eight.)

Page 77: Music Review by Michael S. Kimmelman, June 18, 1987, *The New York Times*. Copyright © by *The New York Times*. Used with permission.

Page 85: Courtesy Great Performances, Thirteen/WNET New York.

Page 87: From THE PROPHET, copyright 1923 by Kahlil Gibran and renewed 1951 by Administrators C.T.A. of Kahlil Gibran Estate and Mary G. Gibran. Used by permission of Alfred A. Knopf, a division of Random House, Inc.

Page 92: From "Singing the Living Tradition," 1993, Unitarian Universalist Association, Boston, Mass. Reprinted by permission.

Page 96: *The All Souls Quarterly Review* is an independent publication of the Unitarian Church of All Souls, New York, edited by Marietta Moskin and Lois Chazen. All publication rights are reserved by *The Quarterly Review*.

Page 118: This entertaining account, by the Rev. Bruce Clear, completes the story of fourteen young Russians' odyssey to the United States in 1990 and their equally difficult trip back to Siberia. We are deeply grateful to Bruce Clear for permitting his story to be included in this book.

About the Author

Dick Leonard was born in Detroit, Michigan, in 1927. In the fourth grade he began violin lessons. By 1944 he was the assistant concertmaster of the National High School Orchestra, with a violin scholarship to the Eastman School of Music in Rochester, New York.

He describes his decision at age seventeen to leave music professionally as "the hardest decision I ever made, but one I've never regretted." He transferred to Yale in 1945, earned a BA in sociology, and graduated from the Union Theological Seminary of New York in 1952.

Married, with two children, he served churches in Bay Ridge, Brooklyn, and East Rockaway, New York, before being called to the Community Church of New York, where he was minister of education from 1959 to 1968.

In 1965 Dr. Martin Luther King, Jr. made his call for clergy of all faiths to come to Selma, Alabama, to protest the beatings of civil rights workers seeking equal voting rights for blacks. Dick answered the call. Following the killing of the Rev. James Reeb, Dick was one of the three hundred marchers who were permitted by court order to make the fifty-four-mile march from Selma to Montgomery.

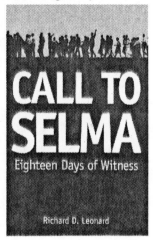

His first book, *Call to Selma: Eighteen Days of Witness*, is the only hour-by-hour account of the now historic five-day march made by one of the three hundred marchers. It is available from Skinner House Press, 25 Beacon St., Boston, Mass. 02108.

Dick was remarried in 1970 to Anna Barr Mason. He and "Polly" have five children between them.

Following his years at The Community Church, he served as development officer for three schools in New York City and as pastor of the Flatbush Unitarian Universalist Church.

In 1979 he joined the staff of the Unitarian Church of All Souls, New York City, as a part-time assistant to Dr. Forrest Church. Eighteen years later the church named him minister emeritus. He continues to serve that institution, particularly doing weddings, of which he has done more than 3000 in fifty-four years of ministry.

He is also an avid chess player, Rubik's Cube demonstrator and lecturer, and has continued music in many forms as an avocation.

The Leonards enjoy traveling when possible, and visiting their far-flung family, spread from New Zealand to Germany. In addition to their children, they have seven grandchildren and four great-grandchildren. They are fond of saying that the "sun never sets" on their family.

0-595-30619-5